Advance Praise for
THE DIVINE INVITATION

"Terri is a lover of God whose heart burns with a fire that is contagious. Her book is full of truth, insight, and beauty all flowing from a wise and passionate woman. You can't read these pages without being called up higher to live a life of love in intimate relationship with Jesus. So read away."

-Stasi Eldredge, co-author of *New York Times* Bestseller
Captivating: Unveiling the Mystery of a Woman's Soul

"Terri has the inspiring words of a craftsman that tap into the longings of every woman's heart. Not only are these pages insightful, but her vulnerability and authenticity pull us quickly into identifying our own heart's needs as women. She then simply guides us through practical steps to unlocking that heart so it can become fully alive in God. Terri is an engaging writer and makes this a great book to read alone or in a group discussion."

-Laura Seibert, Antioch Community Church Pastoral Staff,
Waco, TX, Co-author of *Parenting without Regret*

"We have walked with Terri and her husband Michael for 30 years now in friendship, ministry, and family life. Watching their authentic and dynamic relationship with Jesus up close, through thick and thin, has inspired us to believe in Him for more of Jesus in our own lives. As you read Terri's book, we pray that you too will be encouraged by her life, as we have, to live Fully Alive."

-Don and Julie Steadman, Global Directors of
Antioch Ministries International, Waco, TX

"Living fully alive has been a passion of Terri's ever since God extended her an invitation and a scepter. It's an invitation to take what she has learned and experienced and to write it on a tablet so others can dance with it. To help lead others into a time of fullness that is coming. Her book is an invitation to join a growing community where real transformation in our journey can take place. Where fully-aliveness becomes contagious. Where God extends the invitation to all to dance before Him fully alive, fully His, knowing they are fully delighted in. And together, in an unprecedented season, to stand, laugh, and crush the enemy at the gate. I can't think of a greater reason to exist. Come into this."

-Leigh Barkalow, Speaker - Sheer Beauty: Understanding A Woman's True Inheritance, The Noble Heart Ministry

"In this honest and personal account, Terri brings you face to face with the beauty and power of God fully alive in all of us but most specifically women. Over the years that we have known Terri, she has lovingly delivered to us some of the most impactful messages from the heart of God. I trust that this book will do the same for you."

-Adam and Juli Cox, Co-lead Pastors of Navah Church, Kansas City

"The Divine Invitation is like a wardrobe full of ways to be a beautiful and powerful Christian woman. Terri brings to life the deep relational beauty that provides the models and impact every young woman yearns to have and every older woman hopes to regain. Terri's open and vulnerable story of how God made her fully alive is a gift of life to mothers, daughters, granddaughters, and those who love them."

-Rev. Kitty and Dr. Jim Wilder, international speakers and trainers, Dr. Jim Wilder, author of *Living From the Heart Jesus Gave You, Joyful Journey, Joy Starts Here,* www.joystartshere.com

"If you want to wake up and be fully alive, read *The Divine Invitation.* We stand with Terri as she walks us through what it is like for a woman to be fully alive in a relationship with the Father, Son, and Spirit. Terri beautifully weaves together stories, scripture, and just enough brain science to inspire you to become who you are in Christ. Please accept the invitation and become fully alive."

-John & Sungshim Loppnow, authors of *Joyful Journey,* www.immanueljournaling.com

"I have been honored to know Terri Sullivant since 2003, when she and her husband, Michael, ministered to my wife and me very deeply. Quite simply, Terri is the real deal. No pretense, no simplistic Christian slogans, no making-things-up. And she has found that "radical middle" which balances the ultimate authority of the inerrant Word of God with a supernatural life of hearing God's Spirit and ministering as His co-laborer. Her claims in this book are to be trusted and pondered, and *The Divine Invitation* is the wise fruit of a woman who has walked with God faithfully for a long time. In its pages, Terri presents a very personal, engaging account of her own journey. It is warm, filled with fresh ideas, and teeming with practical application. I especially liked the way she presents and unpacks a host of virtues that characterize the mature Christian life. Ostensibly, this book is a road map for helping women navigate the BETTER WAY with Jesus in the midst of a cacophony of alternative voices. But don't be fooled by this. This book makes an important contribution to a man's maturity in Christ and should be read by men as well as by women. Few books are rooted in scripture, filled with supernatural interactions with God, and told in such a personal, warm, and wise way. This is one of them, and I highly recommend it."

-JP Moreland, Ph.D., Distinguished Professor of Philosophy, Talbot School of Theology, Biola University, author of *Kingdom Triangle*.

"This book will take you from visions to virtues to personal values which will enrich both female and male readers. It is biblical and conversationally connected to lifestyle events which are simple and transferable. The invitation to become FULLY ALIVE is filled with promise and hope."

-Pastor Loren Siffring, MD, Founder of the Master's Christian Ministries.

"As a late 'Baby Boomer' and a convert to Christ from the Jesus People movement of the late 1960's myself, I was still part of a generation that remembered watching Fred Astaire and Ginger Rogers dance with elegance, grace, and amazing alignment and choreography. I would sit spellbound as Astaire would lead Rogers around the dance floor in ways in which even their breathing was in rapport. While Astaire would certainly lead, Rogers anticipated every move and moved with him as if they were one.

Terri Sullivant had a radically powerful, evocative, lyrical, and harmonious experience contained within a divinely choreographed angelic visitation in the middle of the night. As a result, she was invited by the Lord to a dance of grace with the Father, the Son, and the Holy Spirit. It was an invitation to the kind of oneness that reminds me of watching Astaire and Rogers on the dance floor.

The visitation left an indelible mark on Terri. It did on me as well when I listened to her words describe the experience. It imparted to her on many levels an awareness of how important first and foremost, she is to God, and how as a woman, she is called to reign and rule with Christ by His Spirit in equality with men. All too often, not only in society, and even in the Church, women have been marginalized, sublimated, and treated as less than the equals God made them to be.

The insights the Lord reminded her of, all rooted and grounded in Scripture, and the graces imparted, all available to every one of us, both male and female, are ours for the asking, provided we recognize our need to receive them. Terri's words will sink deep into the hearts of genuine seekers of truth, be they women that have not seen themselves as co-heirs of the grace of life in Christ, or men who suffer silently because of their all-too-often performance-driven need for significance, to find the freedom to receive by grace the daily impartation of Christ's virtue to live the life He intends. Regardless of who you are, the wisdom revealed in this book, if heeded and acted on, will teach you how to dance with the Heavenly Bridegroom as that Bride adorned for her husband by His grace!"

-**Dr. Mark J. Chironna,** Mark Chironna Ministries,
Church on the Living Edge, Longwood, FL;
Author of *The Power of Passionate Intention, Life Quest, Seven Secrets to Unfolding Destiny, Breaking the Boundaries of the Possible.*

"Some people explain. Some people blame shift. Some people come across as though they live in a made up fantasy land. Some people never seem to grow up. And then there are others! How refreshing it is when you meet someone who lives what they teach, walks gracefully thru fiery trials, and at the end of the day has a smile in their heart that radiates upon their face. I have had the joy and honor knowing such a person, the author of this transparent book called *The Divine Invitation*. The Golls and the Sullivants have ridden the roller coaster of life together for over 25 years. From that vantage point, I can declare, "Terri Sullivant is a great role model for someone who dances in the rain!" Thank you, dear Terri, for sharing jewels from your treasure chest on "Becoming Fully Alive!" If you desire keys to assist you in finishing well, then devour this book. It will satisfy the deep place in your heart."

-**James W. Goll**, Founder of God Encounters Ministries, Life Language Trainer, Best Selling Author of *Finding Hope, Living a Supernatural Life*

"I love story and journey. Everyone has one of each to which we must pay focused attention if we are to live it to the full.

When you add Jesus into that mix and combine Him with the Father of creation and the astonishing Holy Spirit…then story and journey goes to deeper and higher levels of life than we can possibly imagine by ourselves.

Story and journey are about how we process and upgrade our journey with God. I've seen Terri in the post brain surgery times since 2004 walk out her relationship with God wide eyed with wonder in Him regardless of circumstances. The book resonates with truth regarding what happens when we encounter the fullness of God's nature and personality. He initiates His life in us, and we respond to His promptings on the journey.

I love the crafted prayers scattered throughout this beautiful, heartwarming story of a God who loves who we are learning to become in Him, and faithfully provides the resources for the journey we must all take.

-**Graham Cooke,** author of *Coming Into Alignment, Qualities of a Spiritual Warrior, Manifesting Your Spirit.* brilliantperspectives.com

"Our journey with Jesus is an amazing and multifaceted quest that can be exhilarating and fulfilling, and at times challenging and confusing. In her book, *The Divine Invitation*, Terri Sullivant draws from her amazing life story to provide a colorful roadmap for this journey. Her story begins with a powerful spiritual experience that provides a set of signposts to guide us toward the destination of becoming "fully alive" in Christ. She leads us step-by-step through a series of beautiful virtues to arrive at a place of deeper connection and communion with Jesus. This powerful book is full of wisdom and guidance for the journey of life and provides the spiritual GPS to overcome the roadblocks and detours to become the person that God created us to be."

- Dr. Michael Brodeur, Director of PastorsCoach.com
and DestinyFinder.com Author of *Revival Culture, Destiny Finder*
and *Pastors Coach Essentials*, Bethel Church, Redding, CA

"I am personally excited about Terri Sullivant's book, *The Divine Invitation: Entering the Dance of Becoming Fully Alive.* Before I finished the first chapter, I could hear the voice of God bid me, "Deep calls to deep in the roar of your waterfalls" (Ps. 42:7). Reading Terri's encounter with God raised my expectation immediately and stirred my hunger for Him. Throughout the Bible, God frequently seeks to ignite our *personal* pursuit and surrender through his frequent use of words such as *"come," "ask,"* and *"seek."* In the face of such Divine invitations, how can we live with such tepid faith and sleepy souls?

The Bible was not written to merely teach us *about God* but to *lead us to him.* Terri Sullivant has responded to God's call. She has met him and heard him. What she has to share through this book will ignite your own search for God. And as you will learn from the opening pages, to seek and meet God is life transforming. God promises that his life enhancing gifts of grace are there for those who ask Him. Our heavenly Father is a *promise-maker.* Terri's book will lead you to become a *promise-taker!"*

- Steve Meeks, Calvary Community Church, Houston, TX;
pastor, teacher, mentor, author of *Relational Christianity,*
Incarnational Christianity and The Last Great Revival

The Divine Invitation

THE divine

INVITATION

entering the dance of becoming fully alive

TERRI SULLIVANT

NASHVILLE

NEW YORK • LONDON • MELBOURNE • VANCOUVER

The Divine Invitation

Entering the Dance of Becoming Fully Alive

Published in New York, New York, by Morgan James Publishing in partnership with Author Academy Elite. Morgan James is a trademark of Morgan James, LLC. www.MorganJamesPublishing.com

The Morgan James Speakers Group can bring authors to your live event. For more information or to book an event visit The Morgan James Speakers Group at www.TheMorganJamesSpeakersGroup.com.

ISBN 9781642790672 paperback   ISBN 9781642790689 eBook
ISBN 9781642790696 case laminate
Library of Congress Control Number: 2018942370

Cover Design by: **Interior Design by:**
Steve Sullivant and Chris Treccani   Chris Treccani
www.stevesullivant.com   www.3dogcreative.net

In an effort to support local communities, raise awareness and funds, Morgan James Publishing donates a percentage of all book sales for the life of each book to Habitat for Humanity Peninsula and Greater Williamsburg.

Get involved today! Visit www.MorganJamesBuilds.com

This book is dedicated to the beautiful women, God's daughters who will receive much more freedom and transforming grace from God by making this encounter their own.

And

To my family:
To my husband and love of my life, Michael
Luke, Beka, Jonah, Bethany, Thatcher
Lisa, James, Mairin, Graham, Connor, Niall
Sam, Caitlin, Truman, Annalisa, Jude
Mike, Jeri, and Penny
Steve and Rachel

with prayers that every one of you (and those yet unborn) will enter the dance with Jesus, your Savior, and find your way to becoming Fully Alive. You are the greatest joy of my life second only to Him!

To my Ohio family:
To Mom
Jeff & Joanie and family
Dan & Susie and family
Susie & Barry and family
Liz & Rod and family

with prayers that we might all become the people we were destined to be, and that all of you and yours will know Jesus and enter the dance of becoming Fully Alive!

To my Kansas City community of friends:
You inspired this journey
You are my partners in the dance
Here's to more Fully Alive Women's retreats
More life than we've hoped and dreamed of
More living life Fully Alive
To the "Fully Alive" crew:

The Divine Invitation is also dedicated to a particular group of Fully Alive Women. These women had the courage, strength, and stamina to pull off a large Fully Alive women's retreat in the Kansas City area in 2007. You encouraged me at the weakest point of my life to keep on believing for more for all of us. Here's to continuing to become the fully alive, virtuous women you are all destined to be!

Contents

Foreword

As Terri's husband, it's both humbling and wonderful to be able to say that God has used her, more than any other person in this world, to inspire and help me grow and develop, both as a human being and a follower of Jesus Christ. There is no shame in admitting that God uses another person to help make one a better person, is there? At least, I don't feel any!

My fair lady is a radiant soul... a bright and shining spirit... a truly excellent daughter, sister, wife, mother, grandmother, and friend. She is the most naturally "other-centered" person I have ever known. I stand amazed at how she has patiently, and even joyfully, endured and rebounded from varied hardships, adversities, and setbacks to maintain her sweet style of relating, her quiet confidence in and focus on God's goodness, and her fundamental trust in Him. I must say, it is also sometimes unsettling to live so closely to someone especially gifted at discerning light and darkness and who can come to the right conclusions about situations and relationships long before all the "facts" are clearly seen! This gift in her life goes well beyond "women's intuition." Still, she so often lovingly waits for me to catch up to her wisdom from God as we navigate life together. I am truly delighted to be able to share her life, her story, and her beautiful heart with you through this, her first book.

I was in the bedroom that night in 1990 when Terri experienced this divine invitation. I awoke in the wee hours of the morning with a tangible sense of God's presence resting upon me. Terri was already up, in the kitchen and scribing her encounter. I got up and joined her there. I vividly recall how I was wondrously affected by her account of what had transpired in our room just minutes before. Though we both had and have experienced a number of divine touches in our lives, this event stands out as quite special. Terri has publicly shared this experience on several occasions, and those present have always remarked how they bore witness to its message and authenticity.

This encounter occurred many years ago now, but it was only recently that Terri felt the release to write this book. The content and effects of this divine visitation have saturated and been integrated into the fiber of her being as she has been patiently and faithfully living out, in the course of real-life circumstances, what was downloaded to her that fateful night by God's Spirit. Its transforming message has been gracefully aging within her being and has now become a part of her true identity. I believe that you will sense God's grace seeping into you as you read this book with a vulnerable heart open to your Father in heaven.

The Divine Invitation is a fun and easy book to read that has a very engaging style. It's a lot like having a personal conversation with Terri. It's laced with stories, relevant scripture passages, and inspired word pictures. I predict that you will want to read portions of it over and over again and share it generously with your friends and family.

~**Michael Sullivant**, Kansas City, 2018

Acknowledgements

Thanks to every one of you who has walked this journey of life with me, loved me, supported me, encouraged me, believed in me and received this message. I love you all! You helped me to embrace all of life, the beauty and the pain, and resolve to keep my heart open. You inspire me to live life fully alive!

Jesus—The One and Only. You extended the divine invitation to me; You gave me my Purpose and have walked with me all the way. I am Yours forever.

Mom—You told me when I was little I would one day be an author! I never forgot. You and Dad gave me the environment where I could experience the wide-eyed wonder of life as a child, seeing God in creation, which inspired me in so many ways.

Michael—You are the love of my life, my soul mate, and my partner on this journey.

My children and grandchildren—You are my joy and hope. May you make this world a better place by living life fully alive, each and every one of you.

To my friend Julie—You helped me keep my heart alive, walked with me (literally and figuratively!) in the best of times and the worst of times, and helped my heart to enlarge. You are iron sharpening iron, my irreplaceable, steadfast friend.

To my friend Terri—We are **TnT**! You have delighted in me for many years, as I do you. You've helped me keep my joy and hope alive. You "get me," my kindred spirit. Thanks for holding my heart and opening yours to me!

To my friend Anne—You are such a faithful, ever-encouraging, inspiring friend! You challenge me, honor me, and are "there for me" in so many ways. You are priceless. Thanks for believing in me and caring for me and for my family!

To my friend Mikelan—You have been a faithful prayer warrior and friend in this season of my life. Thanks for your love and support—you are a gem!

To my friend Amy—You are like a breath of fresh air, my soul sister. Thanks for your ever faithful, kindhearted, joyful friendship. You keep the flowers in my life!

To my friend Lianne—You have been a trustworthy, loving friend, like an oasis in my life. You are a gift of a comfortable place to relax and just be me. Thank you!

To my friend Kathy—What a beautiful, fully alive woman you are! You are such a faithful, loyal friend, and a delightful partner in this adventure called "New Hope Community"!

To my friend Donna—You sparkle! You are such a beautiful mixture of overflowing joy and deep compassion. So thankful for your friendship and partnership!

To my friend Sue—Your loyal, faithful friendship is such a gift—your heart of compassion and your tears always show the overflow of a pure heart full of love. You are a gift to me! Thanks for trusting me and walking with me.

To my friend Anoushka—You shimmer with the sunshine of the islands you came from! So happy that you and Curt have come back into our lives, now as friends.

To my new friend Ingrid—Wow—what a pure-hearted, trustworthy, generous, and creative friend you are. Papa was so good to bring you into my life this year!

To Kelley "Renee'"—"We laugh so that we do not cry!" Joy and more life to you!

To Sharon—So glad for the joys and sorrows we were blessed to share. Happy grandmothering!

To Gina and Lisa—You've both been angels to me! Thanks for standing with me in faith for my healing and for your friendship!

To Lyn—You have been an amazing giver and were like "Florence Nightingale" fighting for my welfare in the worst of times. I will always be so grateful for you!

To Janet—I'll never forget the picture you had painted with your face as the Fully Alive Woman—it is your destiny! I'm standing with you and believing!

To Renee' Gus—You have been such steadfast family friends, and you give the best Mama Bear hugs ever!

To Cindy B—Thanks for always keeping the most important things the most important things. And I love your big bright smile!

To Carol M—Your joy in in the midst of trials and your sense of humor are contagious! Thanks for standing with me and staying connected.

To Dawn—Our families are connected for life—so glad to be journeying with you!

To Brenda—Thanks for family memories and the MC years of ministry and fun!

To Diane and Mike—Thanks for inviting us to KC! Grateful for the good years and the impartation of the understanding of intimacy with Jesus and prayer.

To New Hope Community—You are a breath of fresh air and such a loving spiritual family—I treasure each one of you!

To Dan Miller and the 48 Days Community—You gave me a new lease on life and my start in coaching. You are such an encouragement always. I appreciate you!

To Kary Oberbrunner and the Igniting Souls Community—So grateful for the way you served us authors! I may never have written this book without you.

To Morgan James Publishing—It is such an honor to become one of your authors, the first of the partnership between you and AAE. I love who you are and what you're about. I so appreciate all of you! Thank you for helping me spread this message farther and wider than I could ever have done myself.

Introduction

Have you wondered why, if we have the God of heaven and earth living inside us, we aren't experiencing more in life? Why aren't we seeing more of Jesus in ourselves, or others for that matter? Are we really becoming the people we were created to be? What does it look like to be *fully me with Jesus in me* anyway, as an individual and also as a woman? What is my calling in this life really about? These are the questions I was asking myself when God answered me in a profound, life-changing way.

The Divine Invitation provides a pathway for women to find what their hearts deeply long for in every area of life, a metaphor showing the way for every woman to enter the dance of becoming *fully alive.* Learning this dance is about developing a relationship with Jesus that's like two people dancing skillfully and gracefully. It's about becoming so entwined with the thoughts, words, emotions, and behaviors of Jesus that the two of you are as one. This kind of relationship transcends all of life, enabling you to live joyfully and freely, come what may. In this book, I am offering timeless truths in the context of shifting tides of perception of what freedom is and what it means to be fully alive women. Wherever you are at the present moment, "fully alive" or "mostly dead," this book will take you to the next level of connection with Jesus and becoming the person you were born to be!

Seeking to artfully balance biblical truth with both supernatural and natural life experiences, I'm telling my own story and the stories of others, inviting you to join in and discover where you are in your own story. The wisdom I am offering calls you up higher, invites you to encounter God yourself, and in turn, to invite Him into your heart to form virtues in you, gracefully making you a virtuous Proverbs 31 woman.

Note from the author: For those of you who like to read the end of the book before the beginning, there's a promise for you in the Epilogue you might want to read now! Otherwise, it will be there waiting for all of you when you finish.

Chapter 1
THE ENCOUNTER

It is 3:00 a.m. one night in 1990. My husband and I and our four children (soon to be five) are sound asleep in our beds. Suddenly the bedroom is filled with sounds and sights the likes of which I've never seen or heard before. I hear the most beautiful symphonic music—perfect harmonies, sounds I've never even heard in the most magnificent symphonies on earth, more like Enya's music, but no words. I am lifted up in my spirit, shaking off the physical feelings of sleepiness, feeling the impact of this very spiritual music. Then, one by one, angelic beings in the form of women wearing white garments appear in the room. By then I am aware that I am having a dream-like experience, but a "waking-dream," an encounter with God complete with lights, sound, and visuals. Makes sense since I'm a very visual person, and my Father knows that. By visiting me in this encounter, He was answering a question I'd recently been posing to him over and over again: "What does it look like to be fully me with Jesus in me?" One thing I knew for sure, His answer was not something I could make up!

| "What does it look like to be fully me with Jesus in me?" |

Back to the women who were one by one entering into the scene in my room. All were dressed in white, all gracefully dancing to the symphony of sound in the background. Each one had a name tag pinned to her dress, much like we would wear at a women's meeting or retreat. But these names were all symbolic of something. Their names represented a particular quality of virtue they carried within them. All of them had a beautifully wrapped gift in their hands. Each woman danced up to me and gave me her beautifully wrapped gift, simply pressing it into my chest, into my heart. With each gift, I tangibly felt the impartation of virtue, and my instant response was to make room for this gift in my heart. I somehow reached into my chest and pulled out a crumpled old rag or cloth, and handed it to her. Each one seemed delighted to have received it for some reason!

Here are the names of the women in the line-up:

- Merry Heart—her impartation was Joy!
- Unfailing Love—her impartation was supernatural Love
- Peaceful Tranquility came next, her gift being Peace, Shalom
- Lady Longsuffering—her gift was Patience
- Loving Kindness—her gift, Kindness
- "Shirley" Goodness—her gift, Goodness
- Faithful and True—her gift, Faithfulness
- Gentle and Meek—her gift, Gentleness
- Ms. Temperance—her gift, Self-Control
- Beloved Daughter—her gift, secure status as the daughter of her Heavenly Father
- Soul Sister—her gift, sisterhood with other women in our Father's family
- Mama Bear—her gift, the Fierce Heart and Loving Arms of a Mother
- Precious Bride—her gift, marriage in life for some, in heaven for all His daughters
- Faithful Friend—her gift, the gift of true friendship
- Pure Heart—her gift, Purity of Heart

- Sweet Forgiveness—her gift, receiving and giving forgiveness, purified of bitterness
- Maid of Honor—the gift of Honor/Respect, and ability to bestow honor on others
- The Lord's Princess—the gift of royalty as a daughter
- Del Gratia Regina—the gift of mature royalty as a partner, by the grace of God
- Fearlessly Courageous—speaks for itself, courage and boldness!
- Personality Plus—the gift of being authentically, totally yourself
- Total Security—secure; free from insecurity
- Graceful Dancer—graciousness, ability to live in and give grace
- Timeless Beauty—the gift of beauty from the inside out
- Grateful (on her back was written Appreciated)—the gift of gratitude
- Job's Sister—being tried by fire, emerging "better not bitter"
- Unsinkable Hope—the Hope that does not disappoint of Romans 5:5
- Passionate Sage—the gift of wisdom and passion combined

After they had all given their gifts, they stepped aside. A hush filled the room followed by a sense of anticipation. One last woman came into the room. Her presence filled the entire place. Her countenance was so bright that she lit up the whole atmosphere around her. She was a bit intimidating because of the power and authority she carried. But the most powerful thing about her was the love she exuded. Her name was "FULLY ALIVE."

❙   She was FULLY ALIVE in Jesus and He in her.   ❙

She was fully alive in Jesus and He in her. She was standing tall, laughing out loud, and crushing a serpent's head under her feet.

She was the *composite* of all the others, a woman who was truly a great soul, an overcomer, able to fully live and give from the abundance within her. She was the epitome of Christ formed in a woman who was fully herself. She was "redeemed Eve," who had finally crushed the serpent's head under her feet (Gen. 3:15). As I pondered this analogy of Eve, I realized that it was the serpent's THINKING (which is in his head) that she had overcome, the very same poisonous thinking he had injected into her mind in the Garden of Eden. Jesus began to reverse the effects of that poison that exists in Eve's daughters when He died on the cross. He took the poison upon Himself and mysteriously became the antidote. When we receive Him, we also receive the "antivenin" (antidote), which makes the reversal of the serpent's thinking in us possible. The woman named "Fully Alive" symbolized the promise of complete recovery and redemption. She overcame and stood in a new place of dominion, by His grace and her determination to believe the truth in every part of her soul.

The message of this encounter with "Fully Alive" is about receiving the "grace packages" God offers us in the midst of the events, pressures, and pains of life. Names are powerful—they speak of our identity and nature. We need His grace to reject the lies and false names communicated to us through those events by the enemy of our souls. In these grace packages we also receive truth and new names to redefine ourselves according to the truth and align ourselves with Christ in us. There is no end to this process. We continue in it as long as we live. He's given us a lifelong supply of "make-overs" free of charge—no earning or deserving, just because He loves us so.

I am overjoyed to think that this is the destiny He's offering all of His beautiful daughters if we dare to hope for it!

As I have pondered all of this in the years since this vision was given to me, I understand this: what Jesus looks like in me is the alignment of 1) Jesus' attributes, character, and fruits of the spirit, that are true for everyone He lives in; 2) Me being my true self. He lives in ME, and me being, my truest self, with all the qualities of personality, strengths, and gifting that are uniquely "mine." That includes me being a woman!; 3) Living in right relationship with others, in love, as Jesus did.

So the right alignment with Jesus, in me, in right relationship with other people, after being transformed by the "grace-gift-exchange" described in this experience, shows the perfect countenance of Jesus in an individual. He looks like me, I look like Him, and the love I have for other people comes from that beautiful union. This brings great glory to God!

"The glory of God is man fully alive."
-St. Iranaeus, 2nd century AD

There are so many "God-encounters" described in the Bible! I believe these are examples to instruct us through the truth they communicate. I also believe they are there to show us the kinds of encounters God wants to give us all. The Bible is the written Word of God that speaks truth and life into us. It then unites with the Living Word of God, Christ in us, to apply and amplify that truth and life. The Holy Spirit counsels and inspires us to take it from mental assent, to integration in the core of our being, then into inspired action.

"Are you tired? Worn out? Burned out on religion? Come to me. Get away with me and you'll recover your life. I'll show you how to take a real rest. Walk with me and work with me—watch how I do it. Learn the unforced rhythms of grace. I won't lay anything heavy or ill-fitting on you. Keep company with me and you'll learn to live freely and lightly." Matt 11:28-30 MSG

Chapter 2
THE BACKSTORY

As I write this book, I am reflecting back on my life and particularly what I've seen as a woman turning 18 in the '70s through the present, at age 63 in 2018. Wow, so much has changed!

I "met" Jesus at age 19 in January of 1974 while attending Miami University in Oxford, Ohio. During the first week of my sophomore year, a young woman who'd lived in my freshman dorm came bounding up to me and said, "Terri, I've got to tell you about what has happened to me. I invited Jesus Christ into my life and He has totally changed me!" I took one look at her radiant face and the fire dancing in her eyes and thought to myself, "I believe you! I can see it!" During freshman year she had been a bit reserved, withdrawn, and not so happy. This person was observably, tangibly different!

What she didn't know at the time was that I had been praying to God, asking Him to show me my Purpose. I mean that "capital P" big purpose of my life, the reason I'm here on planet Earth. I believed when I saw this young woman and heard her story. He was indeed answering that prayer. She was a sign posted by God directing me to Jesus where I would discover the most important, foundational part of what I had been searching for.

I grew up on a farm in western central Ohio near a little town called Mechanicsburg. My dad had a master's degree in agriculture and animal husbandry from Ohio State University. He owned a business called The P.E. Bline Land Co., a farm management company that served owners of large farms who didn't reside on them. We lived on our own working family farm, where we raised crops and livestock. I was in 4-H from elementary grades through high school, learning how to sew, how to raise animals to sell for profit at the county fair, and my favorite of all, learning to ride and show my horse. I've always loved horses. If I were an animal, I would be a horse! They are a symbol of beauty, strength, and freedom, some of the qualities I most want to embody in life.

I always believed in God. We had over a hundred acres of land on the home farm and it was a huge playground for our family of five kids. I was the oldest of the five. When we weren't in school, in activities, or doing chores, we would be out roaming the land, the woods, and the streams, without a care in the world. We acted out our make-believe dramas for hours on end. Often, when I was by myself, I would marvel at creation. I was in awe of the intricacies of nature. I remember laying in a field in the summertime watching ants on an anthill, amazed at how they all seemed to know exactly what to do, where they were going, and how to self-organize their community above and below ground. They could even carry things as big as or bigger than themselves, dragging these objects below ground for storage. How did they know to do these things? There couldn't be a very big brain in those little heads! Clearly, they were designed with an innate understanding of what they were meant to do here on planet Earth. I intuitively knew that there was an amazing, intelligent creator behind all of creation. All the beauty, diversity, and resiliency of creation certainly was not some random cosmic accident! I was a "Romans 1 believer":

I was a "Romans 1" believer.

"For since the creation of the world God's invisible qualities–his eternal power and divine nature–have been clearly seen, being understood from what has been made, so that people are without excuse." Romans 1:20 NIV

If you've ever seen the movie "Hoosiers," you will understand my life at that time. It was a much simpler way of living, much less complicated than big city life and life in general today. There weren't a lot of huge issues in my life. I had a ton of fun, was successful and popular in school. For the most part, I was a good kid and happy most of the time. I was a born optimist. There were typical teenage heartaches with boys, angst over cheerleading tryouts or big tests in school, insecurities about how I looked and the like, but life was good most of the time.

At home, the hardest trial in my life was my dad. He was an amazing person and achieved so much in his lifetime. He had many wonderful qualities and provided a great life for our family. I greatly honor him. However, he hadn't been healed from his own inner wounds from childhood, so he would erupt in random outbursts of anger that kept us all feeling like we lived next door to a volcano. You never knew when or why he would suddenly erupt and spew angry words everywhere. It was very confusing and painful. Though my sufferings were minor compared to many, they were big to me at the time. They made me aware of the pain and suffering in this world.

Television burst onto the cultural scene in my elementary school years. In keeping with the rest of the world, our family got a little black and white TV. Along with Mickey Mouse and Leave it to Beaver, I heard the news on TV for the first time, making me aware of many difficult tribulations in this wide world. I began to be aware in my elementary, junior high, and high school years that the world was a broken place with a great deal of suffering in it. I have a vivid memory of the day John F. Kennedy was assassinated. Our little elementary school canceled classes and gathered all the students around a little black and white TV in one of the rooms to watch a very sad chapter of history underway. All of these things led me to wonder, "How could a good and loving God allow the people He created to suffer so much?" In the midst of my wrestling with this, I had a divine encounter.

I'll never forget the day when I first heard God's voice. I was sitting on the couch in our living room after one of my Dad's angry outbursts, feeling confused, hurt, and angry. It was like a ticker tape of words went through my mind along with a booming voice in my head. I knew it was God's voice, no doubt about it. He said, "Your dad has a problem, it is NOT your fault, and YOU WILL FIND A BETTER WAY."

I felt a sense of awe and wonder at what had happened to me. My heart and soul did an "about-face" and a "salute" to the One who said it to me. I knew it was God. I knew that He saw me, that He cared about me, and that He wanted to do something about what was going on in my life. I also knew He was beckoning me to turn toward Him and follow Him. I also knew He was going to show me the BETTER WAY. I didn't really have a clue what that meant but I knew because God said it, that there was A BETTER WAY to be found, and I was determined to find it.

> I knew it was true because God said it.
> There was A BETTER WAY to be found, and I was determined to find it.

I believe that I "imprinted" to God, my Father in Heaven, that day. Here's a definition of "imprinting" regarding mammals I found in an online dictionary: "... a form of learning in which a very young animal fixes its attention on the first object with which it has visual, auditory, or tactile experience and thereafter follows that object."[1] That's what happened to me in that encounter with God in my childhood many years ago. The connection has held strong and true for the past 54 years.

That same summer on the farm, our beagle dog Jake came marching into the yard followed by half a dozen little quail chicks marching in a straight line behind him! Apparently, Jake had eaten the chicks' mother and when she was no longer there for them, they instinctively imprinted to him (never mind that he was a dog, who by the way had just eaten their Mom!). This astonished me! It was my first inkling of the power of attachments. I know now that it is the deepest need of every human being to have strong, secure, loving attachments. Apparently, as evidenced by the baby quail, it is the deepest need of every living thing, even if they attach to someone who isn't really safe! Like those baby quail, when one of my primary attachments wasn't able to be "there for me" as I needed him to be, in that void I was able to attach to another. Thankfully I was able to imprint to my Father in Heaven because He showed up for me at exactly the right moment in my life!

Go back with me to the campus experience with the young woman who told me about her transformation when she "met" Jesus. This began the next phase of my journey to finding the BETTER WAY. I saw in her face the radiance of my Heavenly Father's face. I had already imprinted to Him, but I didn't understand or know Jesus. In this encounter with my friend, I saw the same "face" I'd come to trust with a different name: JESUS. It was my first awareness that the Father and Jesus are one. So, I started attending a chapel on the Western campus of our university, taking a step toward searching for this Jesus she was talking about. The next thing I knew I was invited by an RA in my dorm to a Bible study sponsored by InterVarsity Christian Fellowship, a campus Christian group. As I began to meet with them each week, I found myself coming alive when I heard the Scriptures about Jesus and also when I began to pray. I found myself praying all the time, preoccupied by the strong desire to connect with Jesus. I was definitely "moving down the birth canal" but wasn't yet born again.

That happened when our Bible study group attended a meeting in Cincinnati, OH where an evangelist named Tom Skinner was preaching. I was riveted by his story of being a Harlem gang leader, into all kinds of very dark and dangerous stuff. Nothing like the life I'd known! Then he "met" Jesus and EVERYTHING changed! He skyrocketed out of darkness into light, dedicating his all to Jesus. I'll never forget the words he spoke with the persuasiveness of a true evangelist. He said, "Jesus didn't give His 50 percent in exchange for your 50 percent. He gave His 100 percent in exchange for your 100 percent! Those of you who are ready to give your 100 percent to Jesus, the one who gave His all for your life, stand up now." It was as if Tom Skinner was talking to me, really through him Jesus was talking to me! So I stood up, and I gave my all to Jesus. That day in January 1974, I was born again. It felt like I'd broken through into a whole new realm I didn't know existed. Like a baby opening its eyes in this world for the first time, my eyes opened to a new kingdom, a new reality, the kingdom of God. I then knew from experience the meaning of these verses:

> Like a baby opening its eyes in this world for the first time, my eyes opened to a new kingdom, a new reality, the kingdom of God.

"Jesus answered, "Very truly I tell you, no one can enter the kingdom of God unless they are born of water and the Spirit. Flesh gives birth to flesh, but the Spirit gives birth to spirit. You should not be surprised at my saying, 'You must be born again.' The wind blows wherever it pleases. You hear its sound, but you cannot tell where it comes from or where it is going. So it is with everyone born of the Spirit." John 3:5-8 NIV

"For God so loved the world that he gave his one and only Son, that whoever believes in him shall not perish but have eternal life." John 3:16 NIV

Since that day 43 years ago, I've never looked back. Lock stock and barrel, I sold out to Jesus that day and became a Jesus person for life.

What I didn't know until then was that all around me a huge Jesus movement had come crashing like a tsunami wave from the west coast to the east and beyond. I had been caught up in a historic move of God that was so electrifying, so incredibly passionate and powerful that I would never recover from it. I never want to! Ask anyone who came to know Jesus in this time in history; they are permanently marked by it. I know many, many people who came to know Jesus in this time period in our history. They are still going strong in their 60's and 70's and beyond. It was such a unique time in history. I would say I imprinted/attached at a deeper level to God than ever, first to the Father in my childhood, then to Jesus in that Cincinnati experience, and next to the Holy Spirit.

I was introduced to the "face" of the Holy Spirit in Europe as an exchange student. I'd started a Bible study at the Miami University European campus in Luxembourg. One of my friends in the study, Leanne, came across a Christian coffee house on her walk to class and wanted us all to visit it. It was run by Teen Challenge and staffed by a bunch of Jesus people! They prayed for me there and I experienced the "wind" of the Holy Spirit coming upon me. I began to speak in tongues and have regular dreams and visions from the Lord that connected me even more deeply to Him. I finally understood the meaning of "The Holy Trinity." They are three in one, all the same God with three different "faces." If I wasn't mind-blown enough before, my mind was totally blown by then!

In that same time period, the cultural revolution/rebellion of the '60's and '70's was in full swing. Peace signs, love beads, rock and roll, drugs of all kinds, sexual promiscuity, political upheaval, and more were eroding the established values of generations past. Demonstrations of all kinds were being held by sign-carrying hippies, protesting war (Vietnam War), promoting peace, women's liberation, or whatever cause they were stirred up about. There were also Jesus people carrying signs that said, "One Way Jesus Christ." I was now one of them even though I never carried that sign. I *believed* that sign. Jesus people wore clothes similar to what others were wearing (i.e. bell bottoms, tie-died shirts, peace jewelry), they had some of the same lingo, and they liked some of the same kinds of music. But they just didn't act the same way. They had found A BETTER WAY, and so had I.

As I mentioned before, one of the aspects of this cultural revolution was the Women's Lib movement. Some of the extreme things I remember about it were women burning their bras, disdaining men and marriage, and banding together in "goddess worship." These had no appeal to me whatsoever. I don't see these types of things working toward the common good of society at all. There were, however, some good aspects of this movement having to do with appealing for equal pay and status in the workplace. Gaining entrance into professions that had been male dominated in the past was another result of their fight for equality. There were many injustices women had suffered in their homes and in the workplace that were exploding now in a full-blown display of outrage. They made their voices heard. Some good changes resulted, some bad ones too. I felt that women were selling themselves out to a wrong kind of equality with men that eradicated some of the best parts of our femininity. Feminism is not the same as femininity (more on that later).

I was too young then to understand much of what Women's Libbers were so upset about. The way they were going about it was a real turn-off for me. I had grown up with a kind, faithful, stable mother who was a great homemaker, wife, and mother. During our youngest years, she did that full time. In later years, from the time I was in 5th grade on, she also worked with my Dad in his business doing communications, bookkeeping, and public relations for the company from an office in the front part of our home. Since his business office was in our home, she could work from home as well as attending to all the responsibilities of raising five kids. No small task! As I observed my Mom being fully available to her family and still balancing a part-time career, I decided those values were the ones I also wanted for myself. She exemplified the true nobility of womanhood, the kind of femininity which I esteem.

I wasn't yet at the same stage of maturity as my Mom. I had more growing up to do. I was finishing college and getting more and more involved in the Christian community at my college campus. There was a fiery young man, a follower of Jesus, who became well-known on campus for standing up on a "soapbox" of sorts and publicly debating people of other religions. He was even invited to a sociology class on "Social Deviancy" to talk about what he was standing for and against. He said, "I don't mind going a different way in the midst of a society that's going the wrong direction." I admired him greatly. He was involved in InterVarsity Christian Fellowship as well, and then started another student fellowship called The Upper Room Fellowship. It met in the upper room of the City Hall in Oxford, Ohio. Of course, it was a reference to the Upper Room in Scripture when the Holy Spirit came upon all the disciples of Jesus after His death on the cross (Acts 2).

I joined this Upper Room Fellowship after a summer abroad in southern France and North Africa with an InterVarsity program called "Student Training in Missions." I had been greatly inspired in my year of study overseas about the purposes of God in the whole world. I saw how big His plan was, how big His heart was for the people of the world. I wanted to be a part of taking the message about Jesus to other nations. I also wanted to serve God in the best way possible, and I thought being a foreign missionary was probably absolutely the best thing I could do for Him. So, that summer in 1976, I worked alongside full-time missionaries in French speaking nations, France and Algeria, since I had studied French in college and could (sort of) speak the language.

One night, I was lying down in a little cot on a mission compound in Algeria along the coast of the Mediterranean. Our group had been up in the mountains that day among the Berber people, many of them had never heard about Jesus. They lived in huts made of bulrushes and ran out to stare at us as we walked by. My heart was gripped with compassion and desire to share with them the love I'd found. On my little cot that night I said, "Lord if you are sending me as a missionary to people like these, I will go. Here am I, send me." I immediately heard the voice I had become quite familiar with by now, speaking loud and clear: "No. I'm not sending you. Not yet." I was utterly shocked! I thought He would be delighted to have anyone who would sign up for such a task. He then led me to a couple of Scriptures in Isaiah 30.

"For thus says the Lord God, the Holy One of Israel,
'In returning and rest you shall be saved;
In quietness and confidence shall be your strength…'" Isaiah 30:15 NKJV
"Your ears shall hear a word behind you, saying,
'This is the way, walk in it,' Whenever you turn to the right hand
Or whenever you turn to the left." Isaiah 30:21 NKJV

So, I had my answer. I knew that He wasn't asking me to go to the mission field. This was not my Purpose, at least not now. He was asking me to return to Him and wait on Him, trust Him, and listen for His leading. He had always and would always direct me. I would return to Him, seek His face always, and be led by His Word and His voice; that was the greater Purpose for my life. It was His intention that I would always be led by relationship with Him.

> It was His intention that I would always be
> led by relationship with Him.

I had learned something new—He was more interested in me doing the Great Commission WITH Him rather than FOR Him. We are all called to be missionaries wherever we are, here or abroad. However He leads you, the important thing is to be *with Him* in all you do.

After that summer, I went home and joined the Upper Room Fellowship. It was my senior year of college, and I was once again asking, "Lord what's next? What's the next phase of my Purpose?" The next thing I knew, several guys were asking me out. New thought! Most people I knew were not interested in marriage yet, but all of a sudden several people were getting engaged. So I thought, "Maybe I'm supposed to be open to the idea of being married." After dating several guys and realizing they were not "the one," that guy I mentioned earlier, the zealous preacher, leader of the Upper Room Fellowship, let me in on his feelings for me. I was totally blindsided! He was the unofficial president of the "Bachelor 'til the Rapture" club! Also, he was an expert at playing his cards close to his chest. I soon realized that he was, in fact, the guy I had the greatest respect for, of all the guys I knew. And I was also as attracted to him as he was to me. So we started dating, and six months later in August 1977 we had a totally '70's Jesus-people-style outdoor wedding on campus in the formal floral gardens! That's how I became Mrs. Michael Sullivant, aka Terri Sullivant. Another installment of my Purpose had come to pass and is still going on more than 40 years later!

After getting married, we were invited to apprentice in ministry with a pastor in Little Rock, AR, so off we went to live in the south! It took me quite a while to adjust to the differences in culture. I was a Northerner and had never been exposed to Southern culture and lingo. I bought a book called "How to Talk Southern" so I could figure out some of the sayings and pronunciations of things that were new to me! I quickly fell in love with the people there. Wherever you meet people who love Jesus, they are your family! I was also introduced to something else I wasn't very familiar with: RELIGION.

I was not a religious person. I always viewed faith as a relationship with God, not a set of rules and regulations (still do). *This life with Jesus is never about religion, it's always about relationship.*

This life with Jesus is never about religion,
it's always about relationship.

The man who was apprenticing us had a set of rules and regulations that were particularly harsh for women. We didn't really understand the extent of it until we were in the middle of it. There were subtle teachings that were not on paper but came out in verbal statements, practices, and prejudices that were very hurtful to me. Bible verses were twisted to pronounce judgments on the intrinsic nature of women. And my husband and I were caught in a web of unfamiliar thoughts that we had to wrestle through to get free of the bondage that came from religion.

Basically, the message being communicated was that women are intrinsically more easily deceived, of course, because Eve was deceived first. Never mind that Adam fell just as hard as she did! Anyway, the train of thought continued to conclude that women should never be leaders in church, never teachers of men, and always held in suspicion. Their saving grace was to be in submission to their husbands and male leaders of church, and their only redeeming role in life was to be submissive wives and mothers. I had come from a thriving spiritual community where men and women were equally valued, even in our immaturity. I was a spiritual leader in my own right and I certainly didn't agree that women had a 'corner on the market' of being 'most easily deceived'! I felt very bullied by all of this, and I discovered that *religion is a big bully that beats people up rather than builds them up.*

Religion is a big bully that beats people up
rather than builds them up.

We found ourselves in the midst of what would later be known as "the shepherding movement." I think a large part of it was due to reaction to the rebellion of secular culture. "The pendulum swings" as they say. Some of it was just plain deception in a religious package. And the promoters were all men. We left there after some hard years and some good years, having worked through as much as we could in that environment. There was more healing to come after leaving there, which we worked through in the years that followed.

I had learned some valuable lessons and taken some hard hits. I was aware in a new way that there are pitfalls out there for women in Christian settings as well as in secular ones. *Both sides rip women off. Both proclaim freedom but keep women in bondage rather than setting them free.*

> There are pitfalls out there for women in Christian settings as well as in secular ones. Both sides rip women off. Both proclaim freedom but keep women in bondage rather than setting them free.

I was beginning to understand "what's what" in the Christian life. *True spirituality is not about religion, it's about relationship.* In the words of pastor/teacher Bill Johnson, "Religion is boring and cruel."[2] I couldn't agree more. The life God intended for us is about being 'supernaturally natural,' centered on a loving relationship with God and with people. Religion is a set of rules, laws, a *code* of some kind. Jesus came to abolish this once and for all, but for some reason, people opt for the code of rules rather than taking the time to build a loving relationship with God and with people. I guess we're not all that different from the Israelites who built a golden calf to worship after God so gloriously showed His love to them by parting the Red Sea. When we look at the lives of others, it's easy to see where they went wrong, but not so much when we look at our own!

We moved back north in 1985 to the suburbs of Detroit, MI near where my husband had grown up. He was asked to join a team of pastors in Rochester Hills, MI, where we lived for two years. This two-year time period was an incredibly healing time for us. The white-haired older man who headed up the pastoral team was truly a man who loved people well. He had been a medical doctor previously and left his practice to become a pastor. He was more like

Jesus than any leader we've ever worked with before or since. I can't say enough good things about him, and I'm still so very thankful for this man! I'd have to say he restored my faith in Christian male leaders because I was in need of someone I could see and touch who exemplified the BETTER WAY I had always been seeking. He did that for both my husband and me, and we are eternally grateful. A shout out to Loren Siffring! Thank you, Loren for being such a great lover of Jesus and people. You are a shining star for us!

In 1987, we left this place of respite for Kansas City, accepting an invitation to pastor a large church in the metro area. We'd gone North and South and now Midwest! Perhaps symbolically we were finding ourselves in the "middle" where we would eventually "land" in the "radical middle," the "BETTER WAY"—a place of wisdom? After 30 years of living here in Kansas City, I can say we have landed "there," but with a lot of ups and downs getting there.

Chapter 3
THE BETTER WAY
(aka The Radical Middle)

The Better Way Defined

Let me explain what I mean by "radical middle." I believe it is synonymous with the BETTER WAY. This is a term my husband and I heard about in the early 90's through a book called *The Quest for the Radical Middle: a History of the Vineyard* by Bill Jackson.[3] We were in the Vineyard church movement at the time and this really resonated with us. A quote from the back cover reads: "The Vineyard story is a fascinating case study of those that would attempt to hold in tension the great historical doctrines of the faith with an ardent pursuit of the Spirit of God." They too were seekers of the "higher ground" between the two sides. Like me, they were trying to locate the BETTER WAY that I'd personally been seeking since childhood. Most Christian cultures were "either/or," these guys were trying to be "both/and."

We had lived enough life to know that usually the "pendulum swings" and people get caught in one camp or another without the kind of balance that brings a healthy culture. What usually happens is that people react to something unhealthy or unbalanced and go to another extreme of some kind to try to correct it. We've "been there done that" ourselves as well. I believe the "shepherding movement" we found ourselves a part of in our early years of ministry was a reaction to the extremes of the cultural revolution of the '70s. There was such contempt of authority in society that they became overly authoritarian and controlling. There was such rebellion in the Women's Lib movement that they reacted with religious restrictions on women. The truth is, the more reactionary we are, the more imbalanced we usually are. When you're in reaction, you're not balanced, and when you're not balanced, you are usually not at your best.

Most people have watched the classic movie *Fiddler on the Roof.*[4] (There's also a famous painting by Marc Chagall called "The Fiddler" that depicts a fiddler dancing on a rooftop.) This movie is such a great metaphor for the tensions between religious traditions and relationships in changing cultures. The fiddler on the roof appears and plays his song and does his dance when there is a need to find a "higher way," a way that honors the spirit of the truth on both sides and accepts another, better way. This higher way embodies a passionate wisdom, a way of love, of integration vs. polarization. There are limits, it's not "anything goes," there is a time when a stand must be made, and certain things not allowed. That is the nature of truth. All freedom exists within boundaries. What are those right boundaries and what is the "higher way?" How do we avoid pitfalls and reach for timeless truths in changing times? What does love look like and require?

As I look back to my original encounter with God, I believe this "radical middle" is that BETTER WAY He told me about. Ever since, I've been a marked woman, always seeking the BETTER WAY.

I visualize the BETTER WAY like the point or pinnacle of a rooftop. Like the two sides of the roof, there are (at least) two sides of truth, two sides of an issue, that meet together at a point that is higher than either of them. It's about shifting from a thought process of "either/or" to "both/and," arriving at a high point between the two of them. That high point is what I'm referring to here, the radical middle, the BETTER WAY.

"It is good that you grasp one thing and also not let go of the other; for the one who fears God comes forth with both of them." Ecclesiastes 7:18 NASB

Another translation of the same verse reads:

"It is good that you grasp the one and not let go of the other. Whoever fears God will avoid all extremes." Ecclesiastes 7:18 NIV

There's more to this wisdom than just finding a middle ground or compromise between two sides. It's always more than just concepts. If we think wisdom will come intellectually or conceptually, we're missing it.

It's always about relationship, never about religion or religious concepts. Even if we find new religious concepts and practices, better than the old ones, they still fall short.

To get there, to this place of wisdom, we need to come up even higher. As Proverbs 9:10 says:

"The fear of the Lord is the beginning of wisdom; and knowledge of the Holy One is understanding." Proverbs 9:10 NIV

It's about truly knowing the Holy One, being in awe of Him, dancing on the rooftops with Him, in close communion with Him, finding out His thoughts and His ways. I believe the image of the *Fiddler on the Roof* is more than a metaphor for coming up with a better solution for a problem. I believe it's about entering into this mysterious dance on the rooftops, the romance of the dance of knowing the Holy One, being in awe of Him and in genuine, close friendship with him. It's also about caring deeply about people and how we relate to them as they navigate life with us. Jesus cares deeply about people, and when we know His thoughts and His heart about them, we can see them through His eyes and know how we can best love them.

> I believe this mysterious union with Jesus is something we are continually exploring and discovering throughout our lifetimes. I believe this IS the higher way, the BETTER WAY. *The divine invitation beckons you to come and dance on the rooftops of life with our Savior, becoming one with him in His thoughts, feelings, actions—just like a healthy relationship between a husband and wife, only MORE. Much more.*

There is a mystery which in ages past, before the coming of Christ, was hidden. That mystery is this:

"… the glorious riches of this mystery, which is Christ in you, the hope of glory."
Colossians 1:27(b) NIV

Even though the mystery has long ago been revealed, it is still a mystery, and all mysteries are meant to be investigated!

"And we are members of His body. As the Scriptures say, "A man leaves his father and mother and is joined to his wife, and the two are united into one." This is a great mystery, but it is an illustration of the way Christ and the church are one."
Ephesians 5:31-33 NLT

I believe this mysterious union with Jesus is something we are continually exploring and discovering throughout our lifetimes. I believe this IS the higher way, the BETTER WAY.

The divine invitation beckons you to come and dance on the rooftops of life with our Savior, becoming one with him in His thoughts, feelings, actions—just like a healthy relationship between a husband and wife, only MORE. Much more.

"Who can know the Lord's thoughts? Who knows enough to teach him?" But we understand these things, for we have the mind of Christ." 1 Corinthians 2:16 NLT

Jesus Christ lives in us; therefore, we *have* His mind, and it is possible to *know* His mind. That is a process. If we spend time communicating with him, getting to know His voice, studying Scripture, hearing from others who are also learning to know His mind, it is entirely possible. We just have to get comfortable with living in the MYSTERY.

A great deal of religion comes from wanting everything to be spelled out, trying to eliminate the mystery. It's easier sometimes, honestly. Let's just make it all black and white and live by a code that we feel more comfortable with. It's more about *results* than relationship.

Yuck! That makes me feel sick. It's how our religious flesh kicks in to take us out of relational mode.

> A great deal of religion comes from wanting everything to be spelled out, trying to eliminate the mystery. It's more about results than relationship.

There are, however, things that are black and white, clearly right and wrong that are spelled out in Scripture. The Ten Commandments are an example of this. To use the analogy of the roof again, these are like the gutters on the downsides of the roof that you don't want to fall into, to be avoided at all cost. There will be negative consequences if you do. There is forgiveness and grace always, but there will be destructive consequences that will cost dearly. If we keep His commandments, we will be spared from many perils.

So as in the analogy of *Fiddler on the Roof,* you can see that the gutters on the downslope of either side are the extremes representing sin. You will want to avoid these extremes and their consequences! Refuse this kind of compromise.

The "radical middle" or the BETTER WAY is not about compromise like the kind of compromise we see in politics. The idea of compromise here is to make concessions that give only partial solutions to both sides of the issue, not seeking a higher way. In this kind of compromise no one is really happy, both sides feel undervalued, it is, at best, a makeshift peace that doesn't really satisfy anyone.

> Finding the "radical middle," the BETTER WAY, rather than negotiating a compromise, is really about knowing what love looks like for you and all the people you care about in your situation. It's about honoring the truth on both sides of an issue and coming up higher to where love is. It's about seeking to keep the relationships bigger than the problem.

As you seek to resolve the tensions between two (or more) sides of things such as paradoxes and predicaments of all kinds, come to the top of the roof and don't get caught in polarization. Commune with the Lord and ask Him what He wants you to do in these situations. In matters that are not clearly right or wrong, defer to Him and commune with Him. Find out what His heart is, what His thoughts are, and what might be a right course of action for you. Speak with others who are close to Him and ask for their wisdom. Then align your heart, your thoughts, and your actions with His. In this way, you remain relational, dancing in the mystery of friendship with Jesus on the rooftops of life. Then you move from there into your relationships with people, to engage with them and find out what love looks like. This is truly the BETTER WAY.

The Better Way of the Cross of Christ

The CENTERPIECE of the *better way* is THE CROSS of Jesus Christ. It is a *radical middle* solution for all our human ills and the provision for all we hope to become. It is the focal point and the fulcrum for absolutely everything. It is the great crossroads where heaven and earth met in the actual death and resurrection of Jesus and where they now still meet in every moment of every day, every situation in life. For me, this is so deeply embedded in my understanding of what it means to be a Christian that it has become an all-encompassing assumption, the cornerstone, the inception, and the foundation of my faith in Jesus.

> The cross is a historical intervention of God that literally changed heaven and earth. It was prophesied by the Hebrew prophets long before Jesus arrived on the scene. It inaugurated the new creation that was the hope, and even beyond the hope, of the ancient Israelites. It can be understood as a *radical middle* idea because it is not simply death or life, but death *and* resurrection from the dead. There is a divine rhythm that weds these two dynamics together in a wondrous harmony. Humanity needed, and still needs, something more than *fainting* and *resuscitating* when it comes to overcoming evil and discovering true righteousness! For deep and lasting change, we need the grace God provides for us in this, the Main Event of all time.

Jesus' death put an end to the power of all sin, darkness, and death. His resurrection was a radical new beginning for righteousness, light, and life. When the Holy Spirit translates and applies the cross to our lives, we are enabled to "die" to all that dehumanizes us: guilt, shame, narcissism, fear, bitterness, greed, racism, sexual lust, and more. When He imparts the power of the resurrection to us, we are enabled to "come alive" to authentic love, joy, peace, hope, worship, compassion, life-purpose, and so much more. Our personal transformation can happen because, by amazing grace, God allows us all to *participate* in the Cross of Christ. God's new world opens up to us and we become a new creation, a new kind of human being, within our core identity. Our true self can now emerge. This personal change goes far beyond embracing mere concepts, doctrines, ideas, behavior modifications, rituals, and choices. It is based in a new secure bond of relational love with our Creator and Savior that provides us with a whole new operating system. As

I have said and will say again throughout this book, it's about *relationship*, not *religion*.

We all know that love is sacrificial in nature. When we are truly loved by someone, we know their love is real because they lay their lives down for us in a multitude of ways. They prefer us over themselves, they give of themselves when it would be much easier not to, they are other-centered, not self-centered. Jesus showed this kind of love in the most powerful way it had ever been shown on planet Earth. He left the beauty and perfection of heaven itself, became one of us, and laid His life down for all people on the cross. It was the most powerful, awe-inspiring, mind-boggling demonstration of love in all of history.

Death is our greatest enemy. It is a constant reminder of the fact that something has gone terribly wrong with God's originally good creation. All major religions and worldviews acknowledge that sin and suffering have infected all humanity and all of creation. Death is the inevitable result of the corruption that entered our world through original sin.

What God did for us in Christ is totally unique. Rather than *us* trying to somehow undo the effects of sin and restore our broken communion with God, He took the initiative. There's no way that we by our own efforts can resolve the magnitude of consequences that resulted from The Fall. God Himself came to rescue us, to restore us to communion with Himself, and to deliver a dramatic death-blow to our great enemy, death itself.

"Since therefore the children share in flesh and blood, he himself likewise partook of the same things, that through death he might destroy the one who has the power of death, that is, the devil, and deliver all those who through fear of death were subject to lifelong slavery." Hebrews 2:14,15

We all struggle with the problem of evil in our world, all the ways it touches our lives and those we care about. We wrestle to understand why there is so much destruction and injustice if there is a good God who truly loves us.

God, who is utterly good and totally loving, humbled Himself and came to deal with evil on the cross. He did what we were unable to do. He took upon Himself on the cross all the evil, all the sin, all the destructive consequences of yielding to the devil and nailed them in His own body on the cross. In so doing, He exhausted the power of evil and extinguished His own physical life. But death could not hold Him, sin had no place in Him, in Him there was no injustice; therefore, there were no grounds for Him to remain in death. The life in Him was greater than all those things, and He rose victorious over sin and death. He was the Lamb of God, slain for the sins of the world. He arose the King of Kings and the Lord of Lords with the keys of both hell and death in His hands. These are Jesus' own words:

"Fear not, I am the first and last, and living one. I died, and behold I am alive forevermore, and I have the keys of Death and Hades." Revelation 1:17,18 ESV

Wow, that's real love. That's our Jesus.

But we still don't fully understand why. Why, Lord, do we *still* see so much sin, evil, and destruction in our world? We may not know exactly why God allows this to happen, but we do know he has a plan to overcome it. Christ came over 2000 years ago, and His arms have always been open to all people in all nations. It takes time for the 'death of death' to fully play out in this age, between the first and second comings of Christ. Through the shedding of His blood, He inaugurated a New Covenant. He also created a New Covenant community of people who were and are destined to embody the resurrection life He purchased for us with His own life. It is our privilege and responsibility to be the agents of this good news to the ends of the earth. By the power of the Holy Spirit in us, we are empowered to spread the good news and to BE the good news in the way we live our lives, bringing the good works of this New Covenant to all people. We are not finished with this work and we have a lot of maturing to do before we will do it well. It is my hope that what I'm describing in this book will help us find greater maturity, to access more of what has been made available to us by Jesus.

> By the power of the Holy Spirit in us, we are empowered to spread the good news and to BE the good news in the way we live our lives.

"For God so loved the world, that he gave his only Son, that whoever believes in him should not perish but have eternal life. For God did not send his Son into the world to condemn the world, but in order that the world might be saved through him." John 3:16, 17 ESV

In 2001, I went on a trip to France with my mom. I learned the language in college, so I was able to help us navigate more easily in the places we visited. One of those places was Sacre Coeur, a beautiful Catholic cathedral in Paris, France. I so appreciate the way the Catholic Church, especially in centuries past, created such beautiful, inspiring sacred art on the walls, the ceilings, and in the windows of their cathedrals. So many times when I walk into one of these places, I am overwhelmed with awe and wonder; I feel the Presence of God so strongly and am acutely aware of the truth He is showing me in these visual parables. When Mom and I walked into Sacre Coeur cathedral, I had one of the most profound experiences ever, and it was all about the cross. Inside, in the front, on the domed ceiling behind the podium (in the area called the Central Nave) is a stunning painting on a blue background. It depicts Jesus standing in front of the throne of heaven, as the King of Kings, with His arms outstretched, reminiscent of the cross He had just been nailed on before His resurrection. Inside His chest was His heart painted in gold, encircled by the crown of thorns that had been on His head during the crucifixion, piercing His heart.

We both sat down, fixed our eyes on this painting, and began to weep. We sat there for an hour, just weeping. The revelation Jesus was imparting there was beyond intellect or logic, straight to our hearts from The Holy Spirit. From then on, my life was marked by a new depth of understanding Jesus and the cross. As this new insight emerged after that encounter, I was aware more than ever that Jesus suffered far more than physical or spiritual agony on the cross. He felt every pain, every sorrow, every grief, everything we will ever experience in any part of our life, in His own heart, mind, and body. He suffers WITH us in all our sufferings, not just FOR us. I knew that before to some degree, but it hit me in a new and powerful way after that day. Little did I know that He was preparing me for the greatest period of suffering I would ever know, which began in April of 2004. More about that later in the section called "Job's Sister."

That picture had all of the elements of the salvation Jesus offers us. It symbolized the death He died on the cross, the resurrection, and subsequent seating on the throne of heaven as the King of Kings, to signify that He reigns over death and life. It enabled me to engage with the mystery of all Jesus did and still does in and through the cross. It metaphorically communicated the inexplicable pain of heart He feels night and day for all generations past, present, and future. His heart as well as His body has been pierced with the sufferings of mankind. If we are to fully know Him, so will ours. I saw also in His outstretched arms on that painting the open-armed welcome He communicated to all mankind to come and share in the fellowship of His sufferings. If we identify with Him in the sufferings caused by the intrusion of death into our world and lives, we will also share in the overcoming and the joy of His resurrected life. The apostle Paul says this:

"Indeed, I count everything as loss because of the surpassing worth of knowing Christ Jesus my Lord. For his sake I have suffered the loss of all things and count them as rubbish, in order that I may gain Christ and be found in him, not having a righteousness of my own that comes from the law, but that which comes through faith in Christ, the righteousness from God that depends on faith–that I may know him and the power of his resurrection, and may share his sufferings, becoming like him in his death, that by any means possible I may attain the resurrection from the dead." Phillipians 3:8-11

It is my prayer for all of you that you will powerfully be able to engage the mystery of the cross yourselves and be transformed by it.

There is no real transformation without the cross. It is the master key to unlocking our prisons and releasing the resurrection life available to us. It is the "nuclear power" of transformation, the epicenter of true and lasting change, now and always. Jesus through the cross empowers us to change *"from glory to glory"* as it says in 2 Corinthians 3:18. That means going through death and resurrection over and over again throughout our lifetime to restore to us all that sin robbed from us, to renew us to the beauty and wholeness of the original design He had in mind when He created us.

> "From glory to glory" is not bounding from mountaintop to mountaintop, ever higher. Rather it means that we go through multiple death and resurrection experiences in communion with our Lord Jesus. I wrote this book not as a *self-help* book, but a *Jesus-help-me* book. The cross is the crux of the *Better Way. There is no real transformation without the cross.*

This past week I took my granddaughter Mairin to get her nails painted since she would have the honor of being the "star student" the next week in her kindergarten class. Afterward, we went to Starbucks to get a little treat. We were talking about the upcoming week and school in general. She told me about an incident on the playground when her feelings were hurt. She knows Jesus already, so we talked about what to do when someone hurts our feelings. She said, "Well, I can just forgive the people, then take the hurts to Jesus and He will take them away from me into Himself on the cross (appropriate hand motions were happening here!). Then He takes them up to heaven and changes them into something good and gives that back to me! It's amazing! How does He do that?" I was stunned at the absolute clarity she had about how death and resurrection work, how the cross was the centerpiece of it all, and how Jesus does somehow incredibly turn things for good on our behalf. I just said, "I don't know how He does it all, it's a miracle. But I do know that He does it because He loves YOU so very much!"

The Better Way: the Vocation of Virtuous Women

Now that we've established a clear understanding of what the BETTER WAY is, let's take a look at an either/or issue concerning women. When we come to know Jesus, we become truly free women, free to know and pursue our vocation or calling in life. Subsequently we have many choices about the roles we will take on in each season to live out that freedom. We have to do that within the context of the society we live in. That presents a multitude of dilemmas. I want to take a look at some of those dilemmas we face, keeping in mind that we are living our lives on planet Earth as women and that our God-given femininity is a gift. On one hand, you have secular perspectives of women rejecting traditional roles as wives, mothers, homemakers, rejecting marriage, and turning to careers as their main source of identity and purpose. On the other hand, you have religious perspectives that relegate women to only those traditional roles as wives, mothers, and homemakers as their main source of identity and purpose. Like the gutters on either side of the roof, both of those trains of thought can lead to pitfalls when you follow the downward slide. What does true femininity look like vs. secularized feminism?

In my lifetime I've observed several shifts. In my grandmother's generation born in the early 1900's, women usually only had a career if they didn't have a husband or family. It took everything a woman had to raise her family and do all the work it entailed. I remember when I took a "history of education" class at my university how shocked I was to learn that it was once a law that a woman could not have a career as a teacher if she was married and had a family! When you think about it, it would have been practically impossible to have the focus needed to be a full-time educator when she had no dishwasher, no laundry appliances, and very few cars for transportation. Life with a family was all-consuming with very little time for other things. Women could do lots of things from home, but a career outside of the home would have been very difficult. The women who might be able to do this would need to have the means to afford a full-time nanny and housekeeper! It simply wasn't very practical to be a working woman in a career setting if you were a married woman.

In my mother's generation of the 30's, in the midst of the Great Depression and growing up in World War II and Korean War times, more women entered the workforce than ever before. Have you ever seen the posters of Rosie the Riveter? Many women were forced to work because of absent husbands during the wars. My mom married my dad in 1953 and I came along in 1954. Dad had been drafted into the Army during the Korean War before I was born. So, we moved in with my grandparents in the Columbus, Ohio area. My grandma took care of me for the first two years of my life while Mom worked as a secretary for a local grain company to save up money while Dad was in the Army. Mom liked having a career and she was a dedicated mother as well, but she told me she felt guilty at times for working and not being home with me.

I think many women feel caught between two sides of this issue, back then as well as now. "I love my family, but I also love having a career and what it does for my family and me," might be something lots of us would say.

In my Mom's generation, women with children felt guilty if they worked outside of the home. In my generation, born in the 1950's and thereabouts, women began to feel they might be missing something if they didn't work. Many had lived through the Women's Liberation movement, which brought about an explosion of working women, many of them searching for significance in a career. I felt pressure to have to choose a career, as if being a full-time wife-mother-homemaker wasn't enough or couldn't be considered a "career." I didn't know what to think. I once thought I wanted to become a missionary, then after I got married and had children, I wanted nothing more than to be a wife, mother, and homemaker! I didn't want to be relegated to that as my only identity and purpose in this world, as "religion" might suggest. I also believed I had an identity and purpose, a calling from God, that transcends whatever circumstance and season I'm in at the moment. I wanted to be FREE to choose to live that out as I saw fit, as I trusted God to direct my path. I didn't want to feel "second class" because of the path I had conscientiously chosen, but in secular culture, that "slant" did exist. There was a subtle pressure to believe that you weren't "free" or "developing yourself" if you didn't have a career outside of the home. I believed I was doing my calling in my role as a wife, mother, and homemaker just as much as a woman with a career outside the home might also be fulfilling part of her calling in her career.

I had many careers within my home! I was a teacher, a homemaker, a chef, an interior designer, a bookkeeper, a social coordinator, a writer, a musician, a dancer (my children will laugh about this ☺.) I was also a travel agent, a discipler/mentor of younger Christians, a community servant, a minister in partnership with my husband, and more things as well! Many women of my generation chose careers outside of home. Certainly more did than in my Mom's generation. Some found a way to do family and career with equal devotion. Some did not. Children were often in daycare during the work day. Some came home from school to no one at home, coining the phrase "latch-key kids." Microwaved meals or fast food took the place of home-cooked family meals where the family sat down to eat together, resulting in lack of connection in key family relationships, not to mention a decline in overall health. Divorce rates soared in both secular and church communities in the '70's and '80's and beyond. Single parenting became a regular occurrence in our culture. The disintegration of families caused enormous stress and the "casualties" of the cultural revolution rose alarmingly.

Now in my daughters' and sons' generations, born in the '70's, '80's, '90's, and today, it is almost *expected* that a woman *must* have a career outside of the home. Many still choose to stay at home with their young children, but life on one income has become more challenging. Economic pressures have made it very difficult for a family to survive on one income. It has become harder to choose to focus solely on being a wife, mother, and homemaker for the season of life when children are at home and most teachable/moldable.

There is also a considerable amount of fear about family life in young people today which is linked to the failure of many of their parents' or friends' marriages. As a result, many couples choose to live together before they marry.

To make things more complicated, there are now issues surrounding sexual preferences, which were once hardly even a consideration. It's easy for me to believe that due to the widespread over-sexualizing of matters, this is to be expected. Generally speaking, both generations now living here in the West forgot, or never tasted, what it feels like to be in love with God and to love others as ourselves (the Great Commandment: Matthew 22:37-40). Apparently, The Way of Jesus has generally become a forgotten way. I earnestly pray that we will awaken to love for God and others! I pray that we might model something quite different in our own lives and leave a compelling, joyful legacy of a life lived the way God intended it for future generations to follow.

Why am I telling you all of this? I'm simply giving you a perspective from someone who has now lived six decades of life on planet Earth. Life is and always has been complicated. There are some different issues in different generations that cause pressures and pulls on us as women. The common experience we have as women is that we always have lots of things (and people!) pulling on us, often more than is humanly possible to cope with, it seems! All the more reason to look up to Jesus, to meet Him in the midst of the press, to get clearer on our personal vocation or calling, and allow Him to gracefully form His character in us. In that process we also become more fully ourselves, truly fully alive women. This is how we can avoid the traps set for us, overcome our insecurities, our perfectionism (e.g. Pinterest Mom), or avoid just giving up.

As Christian women seeking to find timeless truth in the midst of shifting tides of perception of what's right or best, it seems to me that the BETTER WAY is really about discovering the heart of God for you and for those you care about. It means looking at the freedoms you have within the boundaries of God's standards, which He has lovingly put in place for your benefit. *It's about finding out what love looks like for everyone in your personal situation.* God made you with a unique, original design, complete with a calling from Him and the gifts needed to accomplish it. Finding out how you can love God, love other people, and honor your calling and gifts all at the same time is a part of that BETTER WAY. Whether to work full time or part time or stay home with your kids full time, is something you decide in concert with God, your husband, other friends if you don't have a husband, and your own heart and conscience. There's no set formula, it's really about what LOVE requires, what will be best for all. There's always sacrifice involved with love. There's always a process of transformation underway in our lives to enable us to love more freely and fully, to be the people we were born to be, to become mature, virtuous women, tried and true.

> As Christian women seeking to find timeless truth in the midst of shifting tides of perception of what's right or best, it seems to me that the BETTER WAY is really about discovering the heart of God for you and for those you care about. It means looking at the freedoms you have within the boundaries of God's standards, which He has lovingly put in place for your benefit. *It's about finding out what love looks like for everyone in your personal situation.*

How might we embrace the cross and become the fullest expression of who we were created to be, as women and as individuals, fulfilling our God given callings? How might we do all things well? How do we find this BETTER WAY for women to be free and to flourish, the way that transcends all other ways? We don't need to strive in our search for it. The work has been done, the way has been provided. We just need to accept an invitation.

Chapter 4
THE INVITATION TO THE DANCE

There *IS* an invitation being extended to women everywhere, to find that BETTER WAY. You are being given an invitation to the dance of liberation unto transformation to the rhythm of grace! Come one, come all! Liberation comes through inviting Jesus into your life, embracing the cross, and choosing to follow Him. Transformation comes by the Life within integrating with your mind, will, emotions, and physical body. It's an "inside-out" make-over! There is a "dance" with your partner, Jesus, that you are invited to enter into every day of your life. It is an invitation to step up to being the beauty you were created to be. It is also an invitation to step out to dance with Him in every area of your life until who He is and who you are so integrated, so entwined, that you move as one.

> There is a "dance" with your partner, Jesus, that you are invited to enter into every day of your life. It is an invitation to step up to being the beauty you were created to be. It is also an invitation to step out to dance with Him in every area of your life until who He

> is and who you are so integrated, so entwined, that you move as one. Step up to *Be* the Beauty! Step out to *Do* the Beauty!

Step up to *Be* the Beauty! Step out to *Do* the Beauty!

Have you ever watched two dance partners who have practiced and honed their dance moves so well that they move in total synchronization? (*Dancing with the Stars*, for instance?) This is how you and Jesus would look dancing together. He wants your life to flow with such grace, such creativity, such discipline, such dependence on Him, that the two of you become inseparable. You move together as one, doing the Beauty! Breathtakingly beautiful!

I have personally been powerfully affected by the book *Captivating* by Stasi and John Eldredge and by the retreat ministry that developed around it. I would recommend that you read it and also attend a retreat if you can. I've read the book and studied it with other women, attended the retreat a couple of times with friends and have been truly inspired by it. My big take-aways from it are these truths: Women's hearts have been shut down by the false messages they internalize from the pains of life. Their hearts need to be awakened again to who they are and how God uniquely made them. The core desires of a woman are God-given and good. Those desires come from the original design He gave women. Stasi says it well in chapter one of the book *Captivating*:

"Look at the games that little girls play, and if you can, remember what you dreamed of as a little girl. Look at the movies women love. Listen to your own heart and the hearts of the women you know. What is it that a woman wants? What does she dream of? Think again of women like Tamar, Ruth, Rahab—not very "churchy" women, but women held up for esteem in the Bible. We think you'll find that every woman in her heart of hearts longs for three things: to be romanced, to play an irreplaceable role in a great adventure, and to unveil beauty. That's what makes a woman come alive." [5]

For your hearts to "wake up," these are the longings that need to be honored and validated in your life. Healing needs to take place for the wounds that have brought disappointment and put a "lid" on these truly feminine desires. You are worthy of being romanced. You have an irreplaceable role in a great adventure. You have a beauty uniquely yours to unveil.

If you haven't already, now is the time to step up and enter into it! Step up to BE THE BEAUTY you were created to be.

Once our hearts are awake, then what? How do we step out to "DO" the Beauty? How do we *do the beauty* without striving and becoming uber-busy, exhausted women?

I remember regularly hearing the phrase: "Beauty is as beauty does" throughout my growing-up years. I think this Bible verse relates to that thought:

"For women who claim to be devoted to God should make themselves attractive by the good things they do." 1 Timothy 2:10 NLT

Moreover, I believe that it's not just "any old good things" we are called to do, but there are *specific* good things God has in mind for each of us.

"For we are God's handiwork, created in Christ Jesus to do good works, which God prepared in advance for us to do." Ephesians 2:10 NIV

> What if we were so connected to Jesus that we actually understood who He made us to be and what He made us to do? What if we entered into that dance I described in the dream in chapter one and allowed those virtues to be formed in us? What if the specific good works we are called to do are aligned with who we are and what our purpose is? And then, what if we banded together, performing good works with the people we love for the people who needed it?

I believe that all of those "what ifs" are exactly what God has in mind for us. But how do we do them? How do we DO that Beauty?

Thinking back to the dream of the Fully Alive woman, I know this: The Lord is giving all of His daughters a personal invitation to dance in relationship with Him in a graceful gift exchange. He's inviting you to the Dance! As God offers us the gifts of virtues that call us up to the nobility we were born to embody (We are called to be Ladies!), we receive them freely, gracefully, free of charge, in exchange for our less than noble qualities. Sometimes it takes some doing, some hard knocks, for us to "let go" of our flawed humanity in order to receive what God offers us. But "life happens." It will try and test us to help us become desperate for what He wants to give us. He has already imparted through Christ in us everything we will ever need to become fully alive, godly women—true nobility (Col. 1:26, 27). The gifts He was giving in the dream are full of the GRACE we need to "put off the old and put on the new" (Col. 3:5-10). When we allow this graceful gift exchange to take place in every area, He leads us through the process again and again. One day we will reach critical mass. The composite work of grace in our lives results in a magnitude of authority and light within us. It then shines through the very pores of our countenance!

One thing I noticed about the "exchange" in the dream was that I was clearly being made an offer of something far better than I had. My immediate response was to receive that offer. Afterward, I gave away whatever old thing was taking up space in me to make room for the new!

That's the way grace works. He offers us something far better than anything we already have. It's free. There's no earning or deserving. Sometimes we think this must be too good to be true. We get jaded by all the ways things work in our world and think, "Where's the catch? What isn't 'free' about this deal?" Or, sometimes we can receive Jesus as our Savior as a free gift but then feel transformation (aka sanctification) is something we earn. The truth is that they are both FREE, as in F-R-E-E!

We do, however, have to let go of something to make room for the gift. We have to get rid of some things we've held onto for whatever reason. Some of them are lies about who God is, who we are, how loved and valued we are. Some are habits that keep us enslaved. Some are fears. Some are forms of Narcissism or pride. There's probably a long list of things you could write for yourself of things you know you need to let go of but somehow haven't or feel you can't. When grace comes to us, we are offered the strength to let go of "our stuff" if we choose.

If you are receiving joy, you may need to
let go of being non-relational.
If you are receiving peace, you may need to
let go of anxiety.
If you are receiving love, you may need to
let go of hatred or bitterness.
If you are receiving longsuffering, you may need to
let go of impatience.
If you are receiving gentleness, you may need to let
go of anger.
If you are receiving goodness, you may need to
let go of your 'bad girl' stuff.
If you are receiving meekness, you may need to
let go of pride.
If you are receiving self-control, you may need to
let go of self-indulgence.
If you are receiving faith, you may need to l
et go of fear or doubt.

See how this works?

In light of the offer being made to you, and with it the grace of God to give you the strength to let go of your "stuff," what do you say? The appropriate response might be, "Thank you, Lord! Yes, I receive it, and yes, I release it."

Many times, it isn't that simple. Truthfully, it is always a process, and God is okay with the process. He knows how bound we are, how human we are. He doesn't despise our humanity; He loves our humanity, He actually did make it! And He became human as well, so that's not a problem for Him. It's the sin and brokenness, the rebellion and stubbornness, the addictions, the destructive behaviors, and the "serpent's thinking" in our minds that are a problem for Him. He knows just what it will take to get us to release those things we tenaciously hold onto. Grace, you see, is received on an "as needed" basis. You need to know how much you need it to get it.

> Grace, you see, is received on an "as needed" basis. You need to know how much you need it to get it.

If you never acknowledge your need, you won't get it. To the degree that you acknowledge your need and don't rely on your own performance, you will receive that amount of grace. And he gives grace generously. As the Scriptures say,

"God opposes the proud but gives grace to the humble. So humble yourselves before God. Resist the devil, and he will flee from you. Come close to God, and God will come close to you. Wash your hands, you sinners; purify your hearts, for your loyalty is divided between God and the world. Let there be tears for what you have done. Let there be sorrow and deep grief. Let there be sadness instead of laughter, and gloom instead of joy. Humble yourselves before the Lord, and he will lift you up in honor." James 4:6-10 NLT

Beauty will come from those ashes! (Isaiah 61:3)

He will release His grace to us generously when we humble ourselves, admit our need, and receive it. Clearly, we do have divided loyalties that cause us to be conflicted within ourselves. The wrestling match described in Romans 7 is about the inner conflict caused by those divided loyalties. Like Jacob, who wrestled with God (Genesis 32) because he so wanted His blessing, we can bring our desire to receive His blessing to the Lord. As we wrestle with the Lord, we lose our performance orientation, our ambition, and our deceitful mixture of motivations. Whatever is there, we get to lose our less-than-noble propensities in that process.

In order to receive the grace packages we need to overcome, we simply ask Him, "What area are you emphasizing now?" Let's say He makes it clear to you that He is emphasizing Joy. In light of that virtue, one of the nine fruits of the Spirit, identify what you are currently holding onto that represents a "divided loyalty." In other words, it's something you are giving more power to than the virtue God is offering to you. Instead of giving all the reasons you feel you legitimately have NOT to be joyful, simply humble yourself before God. Bow. Get on your knees and give up resisting. End the tug of war within yourself. Make a decisive choice! Say to the Lord, "I give up!" There is nothing more powerful than You, Lord, I want most of all to have JOY. I LET GO of my right to be joyless, non-relational, grumpy, negative, and acting like You aren't with me. Forgive me Lord. I believe that in Your presence is fullness of joy, and that You are WITH ME always. I receive your GRACE right now to connect with You. I shift into relationship with You, the source of all Joy!" That's a snapshot of what the "gift exchange" looks like. It's simple. It can be easy, but it isn't always easy "getting there."

Once we have received the grace packages God is offering us and given up whatever is taking up space to make room for them, then we are ready to roll. We can take action that flows from the Beauty that's been formed in us. Remember "beauty is as beauty does"? All our "doing" was meant to come from our "being," from a place of rest rather than striving.

"Are you tired? Worn out? Burned out on religion? Come to me. Get away with me and you'll recover your life. I'll show you how to take a real rest. Walk with me and work with me—watch how I do it. Learn the unforced rhythms of grace. I won't lay anything heavy or ill-fitting on you. Keep company with me and you'll learn to live freely and lightly." Matt 11:28-30 MSG

Here's how these "unforced rhythms of grace" work—they are represented by the dance in the dream I shared with you. First, He leads. Then, you follow. Step by step, repeat. Each step represents one of the names of those qualities in the dream. Which one is He focusing on with you right now? Let Him show you. Ask Him. He knows how to move in your life so that you will sense His leading. You only need to follow and trust, step by step by step. Before you know it, you are dancing, imperfectly to be sure, but that doesn't matter to Him. He's just soooooo delighted to be dancing with you!

As you think about the cultural "pulls" on women I described earlier, think about nestling into Him in this dance and letting Him develop these kinds of virtues in you. This is where true femininity is found. He will lead you into the specific roles He wants for you—in career, homemaking, whatever applies. But it's what YOU bring to those roles that really matters—consider this well-known verse from Proverbs 31.

| It's what YOU bring to those roles that really matters |

...To Become Virtuous Women

"A capable, intelligent and virtuous woman—who is he who can find her? She is far more precious than jewels and her value is far above rubies or pearls."
Proverbs 31:10 AMP Classic

When you are able, I encourage you to take some time to read the whole passage of Proverbs 31:10-31. This woman is a wife, mother, homemaker, and businesswoman. Presumably she filled different roles in different seasons of her life. But what she brought to *every* role in *every* season was her virtue.

Now, I want to take a one-by-one look at the virtues being imparted in the dream and the "gift exchange" represented by each one.

There is so much to say about each one of them! I would have a very long book if I wrote all I wanted to convey. So I am planning to create an online course called "The Divine Invitation: 7 Steps for Entering the Dance of Becoming Fully Alive" where we can take a more in-depth dive into each virtue. For now, I will give you enough to "enter the dance"!

Let's take a look at the virtues each of these angelic women were imparting and receive that impartation for ourselves! Let the Holy Spirit lead you as you read to bring the appropriate application for you personally. This process is not about receiving all of these at once. It's one-at-a-time getting in sync with the rhythm of grace.

Chapter 5
THE VIRTUES
(part 1: Fruits of the Spirit)

"But the fruit of the Spirit is love, joy, peace, patience, kindness, goodness, faithfulness, gentleness, self-control. Against such things, there is no law. Those who belong to Christ Jesus have crucified the flesh with its passions and desires. If we live by the Spirit, let us also keep in step with the Spirit." Galatians 5:22-25 ESV

Unfailing Love
Bearer of Supernatural LOVE

The lady bearing this name had a red heart on her nametag, a symbol like an emoji. Here is the well-known passage from 1 Corinthians 13 describing this virtue, <u>the greatest virtue of them all</u>.

"Love is patient and kind; love does not envy or boast; it is not arrogant or rude. It does not insist on its own way; it is not irritable or resentful; it does not rejoice at wrongdoing, but rejoices with the truth. Love bears all things, believes all things,

hopes all things, endures all things… So now faith, hope and love abide, these three; but the greatest of these is love." 1 Corinthians 13:4-7, 13 ESV

To love and be loved is the greatest longing of the human heart. We were built for this. It is the greatest virtue of all because it is the total sum of all virtues. It is what gives us the greatest joy, fills our souls, motivates us to sacrifice for the good of another, and calls us to be our best for the sake of another. It is essentially calling us out of ourselves to prefer another person above ourselves.

Love has many faces. Here are four ways in which people have described these faces. No doubt, there are many more, but sometimes dividing things into categories makes it helpful to gain a better understanding of something.

Agape love is divine love. It originates in God and is given freely with no earning or deserving to those He has created.

Family (familial) love or natural affection is a unique bond of kinship that comes from being related to one another by blood.

Brotherly love or friendship is a powerful bond of mutual affection and trust between two people who choose each other as friends. It is also a way of describing the bond between Christian brothers and sisters, being bound together by the blood of Jesus.

Romantic love is love between a man and woman that includes emotional intimacy and sexual attraction. In marriage, it includes physical intimacy. Symbolically, it is an analogy used in the Bible for the intimate kind of love that is possible between Jesus and His people. (Ephesians 5:31,32 ESV)

When you read the passage in Galatians 5 about the fruits of the Spirit, love is first on the list. If you wanted to sum them up in one word, it would be LOVE. All the others are attributes of love. The more we love, the better we love, the more mature and successful we are in life. That's what it all boils down to.

The most essential quality of LOVE is that it is RELATIONAL. You can't fake it; you can't operate out of mere principle or code of conduct. It comes from a real connection between you and God, and you and another human being. It is essentially delighting in another person. When you look into the eyes of God to connect with Him, engage His real Presence and Being, and when you are grateful and honor Him, you begin to Love Him. When you look into the eyes of another person with acceptance, honor, and gratitude, to connect with them, you begin to love them.

As I write this, I think of all the people in my life that I love so dearly. I see my husband Michael, my children, my grandchildren, my mom and siblings, my friends, my brothers and sisters in Christ. I feel like a very wealthy woman because I have the privilege of loving and being loved by each and every one of those faces I see.

I remember visiting my Great Aunt Betty in Florida, age 101 at the time. She lived to the ripe old age of 104. She was a lovely and loving person all of her life. I asked her, "Aunt Betty, you have lived such a good life, what words of wisdom would you have to share with me? She said, "Go to church. Love others and do as much good as you possibly can for them. Then when it's your time of need, they will also be there for you." I've never forgotten it. After living over 100 years, Aunt Betty clearly understood that there are ultimately only two essential things everything can be boiled down to: love for God and love for people. I thought of these verses of Scripture:

"Jesus replied; 'Love the Lord your God with all your heart and with all your soul and with all your mind.' This is the first and greatest commandment. And the second is like it: 'Love your neighbor as yourself.' All the Law and the Prophets hang on these two commandments." Matthew 22:37-40 NIV

These two commandments are like two sides of the same coin. Love for God is 'heads,' love for people is 'tails.' The two are one.

> After living over 100 years, Aunt Betty clearly
> understood that there are ultimately only two essential
> things everything can be boiled down to:
> love for God and love for people.

Love is also COSTLY. For the sake of love, we lay our lives down, deny ourselves, and sacrifice much. It involves forgiveness when the inevitable heartaches and heartbreaks come. Jesus paid the ultimate price—it cost Him everything, His very life. But He did it because He loves us so.

I was struggling with a broken heart over some painful events in our church history here in Kansas City. I first needed to forgive and ask for forgiveness, but that's not the end of it. I then needed to find the courage to start over and love again. Whenever your heart has been broken, this is the "two-step" dance to healing a broken heart so that you can love again.

During that time of healing of broken-heartedness, the Lord spoke to me in a dream. In it, John Wimber, the founder of the Vineyard church movement, spoke several things to me. He first affirmed who I am, then he said, *"The only way to heal a broken heart is to fall in love again.* So, come on out of the 'chicken coop' and fall in love with the whole body of Christ, that's what I did." I knew this was from the Lord. I've never forgotten it. Fear of having your heart broken again can lock you into a "chicken coop." It takes courage to make yourself vulnerable yet another time. But it's the only way to heal a broken heart. You'll never totally move on after a heartbreak without first forgiving, asking for forgiveness if needed, and finding the courage to "fall in love again." As we do this, our hearts enlarge, and we are able to welcome people in again.

The only way to heal a broken heart
is to fall in love again.

Lord, have your way in me; enlarge my heart. I receive the grace I need to love with unfailing love. I give you my imperfect ways and motivations, replace them with YOUR perfect love. I say "yes" to finding the courage to make myself vulnerable in relationships, to coming out of any "chicken coop" I may be in now. ABOVE all else, I want the legacy of my life to be summed up in the word LOVE. May the epitaph on my headstone read, "SHE LOVED WELL."

Merry Heart
Bearer of Joy

If you recall from chapter one, Merry Heart was the first woman who danced up to me. She was a carrier of Joy! Let's take a look at the virtue of Joy.

JOY is a feeling of great pleasure and happiness, delight, exultation! It is a "high voltage" experience and often results in a full range of emotions from ecstasy to tears of joy.

"You make known to me the path of life: in your presence, there is fullness of joy; at your right hand are pleasures forevermore." Psalm 16:11 ESV

We know from this verse that Joy is found in the presence of God. We know He is always with us, always present. But just knowing that fact doesn't cause us to experience His presence. It's the act of ENGAGING His presence that brings us into the experience of it—where the JOY is found. We know that joy is relational. In Ps. 16 quoted above, we see that it's a relational connection with God that brings us into that experience of joy. Imagine sitting next to someone you care about, but you never look them in the eyes, rarely listen to them, or rarely speak your heart and mind to them. You would be missing out on the joy of connection with them!

We also see in the following verse from John 15 that joy is found not only in relationship with God, but also in relationship with other people.

"If you keep my commandments, you will abide in my love, just as I have kept my Father's commandments and abide in His love. These things I have spoken to you, that my joy may be in you, and that your joy may be full. This is my commandment that you love one another as I have loved you. Greater love has no one than this, that someone lay down his life for his friends." John 15:10-13 ESV

Joy is powerful and enduring. It does not change when circumstances get hard because it doesn't come from circumstances. We may not be delivered from the difficult situations, but we are delivered from negativity and despair by the experience of joy. When you know someone delights in you, that you are the sparkle in their eye, you will experience joy! And it is contagious! It affects everyone around us and can deliver them from their negativity and gloom as well if they open themselves up to it.

> I always think of happiness as something that depends on "happenings." Joy is dependent on our relationship with God and other people.

It is also true that joy and peace are two sides of the same coin. To quote Frederick Brotherton Meyer, "Joy is peace dancing. Peace is joy at rest."[6] Both peace and joy come from the experience of Immanuel—God with us—and from joyful relationships with other people.

Dr. E. James Wilder, in the book "Living from the Heart Jesus Gave You," says this: "In a child's first years, the desire to experience joy in loving relationships is the most powerful force in life. Some neurologists now say that the basic human need is to be the 'sparkle in someone's eye.' When you catch a glimpse of a child's face as he runs toward an awaiting parent with arms outstretched in unrestrained joy, you can witness firsthand that incredible power that comes from 'being the sparkle in someone's eye.'"[7]

That's the power of joy!

In 2004, I went through a time of suffering, unlike anything I'd ever experienced. Out of the blue, I contracted a rare seizure disorder of the 5th cranial nerve called trigeminal neuralgia, aka "the suicide disease." According to my neurologist, it's the most painful neurological condition there is. I ended up having brain surgery, which ended the actual seizures but there was resulting nerve damage and facial palsy, which took much longer to heal. I was on the couch for two years in severe pain on the right side of my face, unable to sleep, barely able to eat, and unable to "do life." I was merely surviving with the love and help of my family and dear friends who rallied around me. Most of all, I was sustained by the very real and powerful experience of the presence of God. After I was pain-free and able to get up and begin to do life again, I suffered from PTSD due to all the pain and loss of that traumatic event. One of the things that characterized it was the inability to feel, to experience the same range of emotions I'd previously been able to. I think of it like a turtle pulling its head and legs into its shell when there's a threat to its safety. My emotions and relational circuits were "in a shell" of self-protection due to my brain's "fight-flight-freeze" response to this crisis.

I received prayer for healing from a lady named Kitty Wilder, wife of Dr. E. James Wilder, the author of *Joy Starts Here* and numerous other books. They and their comrades created a model called "Immanuel Healing Prayer" for healing from traumas of all kinds. As I moved through two three-hour prayer sessions with her, I progressively reconnected with Immanuel in ways I hadn't been able to do in my many moments of overwhelming suffering. The final result was something I have never forgotten, and it brought the healing I sought from PTSD.

At the end of our time together, I suddenly "saw" with the eyes of my spirit the enormous eyes of my heavenly Father looking at me with great love and compassion. Most of all, I "saw" the sparkle in His eyes as He looked at me—I "saw" how delighted He was with me, how much favor I have in His eyes. As my gaze connected with the sparkle in His eyes, I simply melted into a puddle of tears, uncontrollably sobbing with relief and joy! I was able to release grief and sorrow and receive the joy of knowing His delight in me. I truly am His favored daughter, and I'd never lost His favor. In the midst of all of the trauma I'd experienced, I had felt at a very deep level I was no longer the sparkle in His eyes. I'd been "sucker-punched" by adversity and subconsciously received a message that it must be because I'd lost favor with Him. It wasn't a rational idea. It was very deep in my subconscious, in my gut. The clouds of pain and suffering had kept me from engaging with the sparkle in His eyes. Now I could see it again, I could feel it again, *I had returned to the Joy of knowing that I am His delight! He is always so glad to be with me! And He had never once abandoned me.*

This was proof-positive to me—Joy that transcends all circumstances comes from relational ATTACHMENT, from imprinting securely to our Heavenly Father, seeing His face, connecting to His Presence. It also comes from that kind of relationship with other people.

> Joy that transcends all circumstances comes from relational ATTACHMENT, from imprinting securely to our Heavenly Father, seeing His face, connecting to His Presence. It also comes from that kind of relationship with other people.

Since that day, I start each day in prayer with Him, looking up once again into His eyes to engage with the sparkle in His eye that is always there for me. I always feel His Presence as I do that, and it opens me up to Joy at the start of the day. Whenever I feel distressed, I look for His gaze. Like a little child, I know if I can see His face and drink in that sense of His favor, I am fine. I can rest and be joyful—end of story.

It's normal to feel sorrow, sadness, and pain in this world, and there's no avoiding that. We all pass through these on our way to returning to joy, like passing from nighttime to morning.

"…his favor is for a lifetime. Weeping may tarry for the night, but joy comes with the morning." Psalm 30:5 ESV

God is the source of joy that never runs dry. Staying connected to him as we relate to one another gives us the ability to love others with that same sparkle in our eyes. When we see others as He sees them and delight in who they are, they feel it and reciprocate if they are able. Think about the strongest, deepest relationships you have. What do you experience in those relationships that brings you great joy? Isn't it that you feel they really "get you," they "see" you, value you, delight in you, and enjoy being with you? Relationships with others are the greatest joy we have on this earth, second only to our relationship with God. Investing in your relationships is an investment in JOY! As we read in John 15:10-13, when we love one another, we experience FULLNESS of joy. If you want to receive the fullness of Joy, you will excel in loving others.

So how about it? Will you receive the grace package the Lord is offering you to have fullness of JOY? Let go of negativity and gloom, look up into the eyes of Jesus and see that sparkle in His eyes, let the awareness that He is as glad as can be to be with you wash over you now! Let Joy come into your heart like the dawn of a brand-new day and a better way. Be empowered to live above the storms of life and become buoyant with the power of JOY!

Peaceful Tranquility
Bearer of SHALOM, Transcendent Peace, Well-Being

This lady brought one of the most powerful qualities of life available.

"Jesus said, 'Peace I leave with you, My peace I give to you; not as the world gives do I give to you. Let not your heart be troubled, neither let it be afraid.'" John 14:27 NKJV

He is speaking to His disciples in the context of preparing them for His departure, namely His crucifixion, death, and resurrection, after which He would no longer be physically present on earth until the day of His return. He lets them know that the Holy Spirit will come to dwell in them after He leaves. He knew they would be experiencing separation anxiety when they could no longer see His face, so He tells them they will be given supernatural peace to alleviate that anxiety.

How do we access that peace? It comes through relational connection with God, where we engage Him, encounter Him, we "see His face," see the sparkle in His eyes, and relax inside. On a moment-by-moment basis, this is available to us. True spirituality is about RELATIONSHIP.

> Religion is about a code of conduct we adhere to apart from the relational connection.

This PEACE comes from RELATIONSHIP, *not* RELIGION.

How can we reconnect when we lose connection? Or maybe you feel like you've never really connected with God in the first place. The secret is found in Psalm 95:2 *"Let us come into His presence with thanksgiving..."* It is the practice of gratitude, of thanksgiving, that causes us to enter into, i.e. engage, His presence. Also, in Psalm 100:4 the Bible says, *"Enter his gates with thanksgiving, and his courts with praise! Give thanks to Him, bless His name!"* The entryway, or doorway, into His presence is accessed with gratitude. In the book *Joyful Journey* by Dr. James Wilder, Anna Kang, and John and Sungshim Loppnow, they say it like this:

> *"Gratitude opens us up to the presence of God. Gratitude is a password into our awareness of the presence of God. We specifically chose gratitude because it is the easiest and fastest path to connection and because throughout scripture, God in His wisdom has always encouraged us to give thanks."*[8]

Here's the secret: Gratitude is the password into the Presence! So many things in our world now are Internet based and must be accessed with a password. That analogy fits well here. To access God's presence, which is available 24-7, we use the password GRATITUDE!

Where He is Present, there is PEACE. In other words, wherever and whenever we experience His Presence, we also experience His peace. He is, after all, the Prince of Peace!

As a pastor and a life coach, I use a tool called "Interactive Gratitude" to help people access God's Presence, experience genuine Peace, and overcome anxiety. I will include a template for this at the end of this book. Simply explained, there are two steps:

1. Take a moment to engage with God, and think of something you are truly grateful for, anything at all. Write that down.
2. Listen for God's response. Without judging what comes to you, write that down.

It is amazing how many people come to tears when they hear God's response to their gratitude. Why? It's because you are suddenly aware of His presence in a tangible way, He's no longer hidden. Suddenly, there is peace, and possibly joy as well, when you know He is with you!

I learned about this through the writings and practices of Dr. James Wilder and others in a group called The Life Model (https://joystartshere.com). It is amazing how this little tool can change your life if you practice it throughout the day and keep a "Gratitude Journal," even naming the experiences you have like a table of contents. It's an intentional dialogue between you and God that results in well-worn pathways of connection with God. It is a powerful way to dissolve anxieties before they can find a "landing strip" in your mind. You can go back and look through what you've already experienced and let it be an inspiration for your next interactive gratitude. Sharing your interactive gratitude with others in a group is also very powerful. It's a snowball effect!

"...the Lord is at hand; do not be anxious about anything, but in everything by prayer and supplication <u>with thanksgiving</u> let your requests be made known to God. And the PEACE OF GOD, which surpasses understanding, will guard your hearts and your minds in Christ Jesus." Philippians 4:5(b)-7

Maybe we have misunderstood PRAYER. Many times, we think of it as a monologue, a one-way communication with God, hoping He hears us. PRAYER is intended to be a DIALOGUE, a running conversation with God. That kind of prayer keeps us living in the awareness of His tangible Presence and feeling connected to Him because He talks back to us! All relationships are a two-way street, including our relationship with God. So how about it? How about keeping a running dialogue open with Him throughout our days? I believe this is the biggest key to living Peace as a lifestyle.

Lord, I receive your PEACE. You are the Prince of Peace, and I receive You as my Peace. I give you my anxious thoughts, my fears, my worries. I let them go into your hands in exchange for the Powerful Peace you are offering me!

Lady Longsuffering
Bearer of Patience

Hello, Lady Longsuffering! Her name says it all, doesn't it? To develop the quality of patience in our lives, we do have to endure long-term hardship well. As in, throughout all our days!

As I write this and think back over my lifetime, I realize this: I am much more patient now at age 63 than I was at 19 when I began to walk with Jesus! The first Scripture that comes to mind is in Luke 8:

"As for that (seed) in the good soil, they are those who, hearing the word, hold it fast in an honest and good heart, and bear fruit with patience." Luke 8:15 ESV

Jesus is unpacking the parable of the sower for His disciples to help them understand it. He talks them through the seed sown on rocky ground, on weed-infested ground, and lands on the seed sown in good soil. In essence, He is saying that patience enables the seed to take root, flourish, and bear fruit.

Growing up on the farm, we did a lot of labor in the fields. There was one field I could swear produced rocks. That was its main crop! My brothers and I would go with Dad to pick up these rocks and pile them up, so the ground could be tilled and planted. No matter how many rocks we piled up, it seemed there were always more, and each year appeared to be no better than the year before. It was definitely a job that required longsuffering. They were heavy, and it took such a long time to do that job. While we were at it, we would also pull out weeds by the roots in hopes that they wouldn't grow back. Even though those particular weeds wouldn't grow back, somehow other weeds would grow every year in their place and needed constant pulling. By removing the rocks and weeds, the land became tillable. It would be able to sustain seeds that would yield whatever crop was planted there.

There are many things in life like this, things that you have to do over and over—like: getting up and going to work each day; feeding, caring for, and bathing young children; dishes; housecleaning; maintenance on your home; auto repair; personal hygiene; bill paying. Endless tasks.

Tending to the rocks and weeds in your heart is the same way; things like negative thoughts/speech, resentment, bitterness, impatient attitudes, dishonesty, complaining, dishonorable attitudes toward people, etc. The list of rocks and weeds is long, and as long as we live, we will have to pull them up and dispose of them to make our lives fruitful. It is a painstaking, patience-producing process!

What comes to my mind is this verse:

"... looking to Jesus, the founder and perfecter of our faith, who for the joy that was set before him endured the cross..." Hebrews 12:2 ESV

> For the joy of producing much fruit in our lives, it is worth the longsuffering that is required to remove the rocks and weeds. If the seeds of faith, hope, and love take root, we will bear beautiful, bountiful fruit and be a blessing to many people.

Persevering in the midst of suffering is another description of patience.

"Brothers and sisters, as an example of patience in the face of suffering, take the prophets who spoke in the name of the Lord. As you know, we count as blessed those who have persevered. You have heard of Job's perseverance and have seen what the Lord finally brought about. The Lord is full of compassion and mercy." James 5:10-11 NIV.

It becomes especially hard to persevere patiently when you are experiencing intense pain and trials. There is a promise of a double portion of blessing at the end of that test. For Job, it happened in his lifetime. For others, it may be in the life to come. Earlier, I described the intense painful suffering I went through for two years. The Lord spoke to me early on and said, "I dare you to stand and believe in me for your complete healing." There were many times when I wanted to give up because it was so painful and hard for so long. With the help of many wonderful friends who gathered around me to pray and support me, I made it through and was completely healed. There were five distinct touches from the Lord that brought the pain level down from ten to nine, then to seven, to five, to two, and to zero. There were doctors and nutritionists who helped me recover as well. Others who were soul-healers helped me deal with the grief and PTSD. The Lord could have done it all at once. He didn't. Instead, He tested my patience and produced greater longsuffering in my life by doing it that way.

"We want each of you to show this same diligence to the very end, so that what you hope for may be fully realized. We do not want you to become lazy, but to imitate those who through faith and patience inherit what has been promised." Hebrews 6:11,12 NIV

Lord, I receive the grace-gift of Patience. I let go of my impatient, demanding, unloving ways to make room for it. Let this seed fall on good soil in my heart and produce an abundance of patient longsuffering!

Loving Kindness
Bearer of Kindness

Kindness is the second virtue in the list of the attributes of love in 1 Corinthians 13. Kindness is one of those universal values that *everyone* appreciates when they are the recipients of it. Likewise, it is equally NOT appreciated when someone is on the receiving end of unkind words or actions. It is a powerful, life-giving virtue that can turn away the anger of someone having a fit of rage, that can surprise a wounded person into believing in human goodness again, that can disarm another person and begin a friendship. Kindness is displayed in attitudes, words, and deeds. One definition of kindness is "helpfulness towards someone in need, not in return for anything, nor for the advantage of the helper himself, but for that of the person helped." [9]

God is kind! In some religious settings, He is portrayed as an angry, mean-spirited despot, eager to make you pay for your wrongs. The truth is: He has done all the hard work of removing all the reasons He might have to be angry, all our sinful nature with all its offensiveness has been nailed to the cross with Jesus. In His Kindness, He took it all on Himself because He knew we couldn't bear it and because His intention has always been for our welfare.

It was His desire for our welfare and for us to understand How much He loves us that led Him to do all this willingly.

Here are some Bible verses about kind words:

"A gentle answer turns away wrath. But a harsh word stirs up anger." Proverbs 15:1 NASB

"Pleasant words are a honeycomb, Sweet to the soul and healing to the bones." Proverbs 16:24 NASB

"She opens her mouth in wisdom, And the teaching of kindness is on her tongue." Proverbs 31:26 NASB

My Mom is one of the kindest people I know. She is kind in her actions and interactions with our family and everyone she relates to. She looks for ways to show kindness to others. It creates an environment of safety and peace around her that is very inviting. I've watched her defuse anger on many occasions with a kind demeanor and kind words. She makes you feel better about yourself and the world around you. She also walks and talks the ways of kindness in an unassuming way, by example, instructing you to do the same.

Kindness is intentional. It can become habitual with practice. It is contagious. It is one of the greatest, most powerful virtues we as women can embody.

Lord, I want to be a woman of kindness. I want all my thoughts, words, and actions to speak kindly to others around me. I give you my unkind ways of speaking, thinking, and behaving. I come to the cross with all the inferior motivations that cause me to be unkind. I make room to receive the grace to be characterized by kindness all the days of my life. I receive this gift from you today, in Jesus' name.

Shirley Goodness
The bearer of goodness

I had to smile a little at the play on words here, reminiscent of the verse from Psalm 23:6

"Surely goodness and mercy will follow me all the days of my life…" ESV

"Good" is probably one of the most used words in our vocabulary. We probably use it multiple times a day if you think about it. We use it to mean a variety of things. "How are you?" "I'm good." "How was the (food, movie, fill in the blank)?" "Good." "She's a good person." "Good work." The list goes on and on as we determine what's either good or not good.

I'd like to start with the source. The source of all goodness is God Himself. GOD IS GOOD in the truest, purest sense of the word. He is BETTER than we think. He gets accused of not being good almost every day, probably because people blame Him for the evil in the world. The fact that evil exists doesn't mean God isn't good. He created everything GOOD because He is GOOD!

> The source of all goodness is God Himself. God is Good in the truest, purest sense of the word.

I think we would all agree that goodness has to do with integrity, righteousness, and excellent moral fiber. That's who God is, and His children are deemed and destined to be good too! Some synonyms of goodness would be: virtue, righteousness, morality, and integrity. Because He is all those things and more, we get to be good too. Not perfect, but good, because His goodness is in us. We were created to be good originally (Ps. 139, we are fearfully and wonderfully made), and we were redeemed to be good (1 Corinthians 1:30). Surely we can embody goodness because He embodies goodness and He lives in our bodies!

There are many human definitions of goodness that might not include the moral integrity I described above as the nature of God. These human versions may or may not intersect with those pertaining to God. For instance, the popular saying and clothing brand, "Life is Good" may refer more to human experience than the character of God. It's great when circumstances are good, but we all know they aren't always that way.

I would say, "Life isn't always good, but God is Good ALWAYS!"

Because He is always with us, we have the experience of goodness available to us even when things are hard and we are hurting. We have a RELATIONSHIP with God who is GOOD All the Time!

When I think of someone who is truly what I would call a good person, I think of my son, Sam. Everyone who knows him would say that about him! He has a great deal of integrity, moral fiber, and genuine concern for others. He has a strong sense of justice and deep desire to be truly good, truly godly. He is a cinematographer, and in his industry, there are many opportunities for compromise. His strong internal plumb-line has held him steady and true. He has been a beacon of light to many people, and I'm super proud of him.

I have many friends who I would call "salt of the earth" kind of people. They are just plain GOOD people. They know God is good and they choose to be good, rain or shine. They inspire me. Salt is a preservative and I think of it as a metaphor for preserving all that is GOOD about human life and planet Earth. Also, salt makes you thirsty, so when you taste the life of a salty person, it makes you thirsty for the goodness they have. In addition, it enhances what's already good and makes it better, as salt does with food.

Lord, I want to be a "salt of the earth" kind of person, full of goodness, rain or shine. I receive your GOODNESS in exchange for my lack thereof. May it be said of me, "Surely goodness and mercy have followed me all the days of my life…" May the fruit of my life leave a trail of good fruit and saltiness wherever I go.

Faithful and True
Bearer of faithfulness

When you think of a faithful person, what do you think of? What comes to my mind is a person who is steadfast, loyal, devoted, unwavering in commitment to God, to other people, and to what they have promised. The word itself is a compound word meaning "full of faith," which leads to the conclusion that you can't have this virtue without being full of faith!

"Faithfulness is the concept of unfailingly remaining loyal to someone or something and putting that loyalty into consistent practice, regardless of extenuating circumstances." [10]

Today, I'm so thankful for the faithfulness of my husband! As I write this, it is Father's Day, and I am very aware of how his faithfulness to me as my husband and as a daddy to our five kids has blessed my life and the lives of our children. He has been uncompromising in his fidelity to me in marriage, so much so that I never worry about it. Never have to. His faithfulness to our children has given them a security in life that is a priceless gift. He has provided for and cared for us all faithfully. I know the source of his faithfulness is His relationship with our Faithful God. He has known Jesus since his college years and has been unwavering in His loyalty to knowing and serving Him. My children have not struggled greatly to trust the faithfulness of God because of their Daddy's faithfulness to them. Michael has been trustworthy because He has known the trustworthiness of our Faithful God for many decades now. He knows that our God is Faithful and True!

Life is fragile, but God is faithful. In the book of Lamentations, the writer proclaims what he has found to be true about God in the midst of severe trials:

"The faithful love of the Lord never ends! His mercies never cease. Great is His faithfulness; His mercies begin afresh each morning. I say to myself, "the Lord is my inheritance; therefore, I will hope in Him!" Lamentations 3:22-24 NLT

Life is fragile, but God is faithful.

Dear Lord, I know You alone are 100 percent Faithful and True to me even if all others have failed me. I yield my doubts, my fear of trusting, and my pain to You and receive the relationship with You that will fulfill me and secure me. I choose to receive your faithfulness to me, so I can in turn be faithful to You and to others. Let this gift come into my heart today!

Gentle and Meek
Bearer of gentleness/meekness

Some descriptors of the quality of gentleness include: "mild in temperament or behavior, kind or tender, not harsh or severe." Meekness is very similar to gentleness. It is having or showing a quiet and gentle nature and not being given to fighting or arguing. It includes being humble and teachable. For years, I've heard this verse and pondered it:

"Now the man Moses was very meek, more than all people who were on the face of the earth." Numbers 12:3 ESV

Wow! I want to be like him! But what does that mean?

Moses was a very strong man, so his meekness and gentleness did not mean he was a weak person. He was simply restrained, not perfectly, of course, as evidenced by certain instances in the Bible where he failed the test, but in spite of imperfect performances, he went down in history as the meekest, most humble man on the face of the planet!

Good thing for us. It is not our perfect performance but our *usual way of behaving and relating* that characterizes us as "gentle" or "meek."

> It is not our perfect performance but our *usual way of behaving and relating* that characterizes us as "gentle" or "meek."

I think of the horse as a good symbol of gentleness and meekness. A horse is a great picture of "strength harnessed" or strength under control. When a horse has been tamed and trained, it will submit to the saddle and bridle and willingly follow the lead of its master. When the horse has become gentle and meek, it becomes most valuable to those it serves. It has great strength, but strength that has been harnessed in order to live out its greatest potential in service to others.

As I write today, I am at the farm, my childhood home. My brother and I went out to the barnyard yesterday to see his new herd of Shorthorn beef cows lounging there, swatting flies in the heat of the day. Among them was a white Shorthorn bull with a ring in his nose. Generally, this kind of creature conjures up some fear in me due to bad experiences in the past with bulls charging me if I stepped into a pasture they believed to be their territory! Much to my surprise, this bull was very gentle, had been trained for show, and could be easily led by halter or by the ring in his nose. I could actually pet him and scratch his head! It was a treat to get to do that. I felt myself totally relax inside, and the normal fears subsided. I thought, "This is what happens inside of you when you are around a gentle, meek person. It is disarming, relaxing, and you can heave a sigh of relief." So nice! This bull was anything but weak; he was very bulky and strong. He was capable of doing serious damage. He still incited a healthy respect! But because he had submitted to training, he had become very gentle and meek, a rarity among his kind. (I named the bull Ferdinand ☺)

We are not weaklings. God has given each of us great strengths that can be used for good or evil; we can choose.

Lord, today I choose to humble myself to receive the grace-gift of gentleness and meekness. I release my natural desires to control my own life, to throw my strength around, to overpower, to be harsh in word and deed. I don't want these things; I want to be like you and like Moses, gentle and meek.

Ms. Temperance
Bearer of self-control

According to Psychology Today, self-control is something that psychologists have defined as "what separates us from the rest of the animal kingdom, thanks to our large prefrontal cortex. It is the ability to subdue our impulses to achieve longer-term goals. Rather than responding to impulses, we can plan, evaluate alternative actions, and often enough, avoid doing things we'll later regret."[11]

We are capable of much more self-control than we may think as human beings. How much more are we capable of self-control when we are allowing the Holy Spirit within us to strengthen us when we are tempted? Even more, we are empowered to exercise self-control when we have someone or something we value more than the fulfillment of our impulses to focus on!

> …we are empowered to exercise self-control when we have someone or something we value more than fulfillment of our impulses to focus on!

Consider these verses of Scripture:

"...for God gave us a spirit not of fear, but of power and love and self-control." 2 Timothy 1:7 ESV

"Better to be patient than powerful; better to have self-control than to conquer a city." Proverbs 16:32 NLT

"Like a city whose walls are broken through is a person who lacks self-control." Proverbs 25:28 NLT

"The Spirit of God, who raised Jesus from the dead, lives in you. And just as God raised Christ Jesus from the dead, he will give life to your mortal bodies by this same Spirit living within you." Romans 8:11 NLT

The picture I have in my mind right now is of a pet Corgi dog named Lucius who belonged to our daughter and her family. He has gone on to "doggie heaven" now, God rest his soul, but he demonstrated some serious self-control in his lifetime! Lisa's husband, James, had balanced a dog treat straight across his nose and commanded him to sit still and resist eating it. That dog sat there, unflinching, until he was released to eat the treat, which he PROMPTLY did when he got the signal! Amazing! It was such a great example of how he valued pleasing my daughter and son-in-law over indulging himself, and how he received a reward for doing so.

I believe we can forgo many of our wants and even needs at times in favor of pleasing the One we love and serve. Because of the loving relationship Jesus has offered us, it's well worth it. We can deny ourselves, refusing to give into temptations that would detract from that relationship. No need to beat yourself up for imperfect performance. Remember, it's not about religion, it's about relationship!

Likewise, in light of the love we have for our family and friends, we can exercise great self-control so that we can offer them more—more of ourselves, more of what they need. It's beautiful to watch how parents deny themselves to offer all they possibly can to their children. They give until it hurts and then give more. Real friends are like this, too. Sacrificing their convenience on your behalf. Giving up their time, energy, resources for your benefit. Denying themselves for the sake of love. That's the best motivator for this virtue.

Nothing has the right to control us unless we let it. Unfortunately, we have all allowed other things control us, things that are not good for us or those around us. Thankfully, He knows our frailties and has given us extra grace when we need it! It is available in unlimited supply.

Nothing has the right to control us unless we let it.

"For we do not have a high priest who is unable to sympathize with our weaknesses, but one who in every respect has been tempted as we are, yet without sin. Let us then with confidence draw near to the throne of grace, that we may receive mercy and find grace to help in time of need." Hebrews 4:15, 16 ESV

Lord, I come to you today desiring your grace, knowing that it is received on an "as-needed" basis! I know I need more grace to live a life of self-control under the powerful influence of your spirit. I release my lack of self-control. I give you my propensity to let other things control me, things that distract me from that reward—that wonderful friendship with you and others I love. I want that more! So, I let go of those other things and receive the grace-gift of self-control today.

Chapter 6
THE VIRTUES
(part 2: Relationships/Roles)

Beloved Daughter
Bearer of the Father's love

We all share this favored relational status. We are all beloved daughters of our Father in heaven. Our first priority relationally is to become secure and grounded in this relationship. It is the foundation for all other relationships in life. Once you have encountered the Father's love for you and have experienced it in the depths of your soul (mind, emotions, personality), you will have fulfilled one of the deepest needs and desires we have as women—to know we are unconditionally accepted, deeply loved, and cherished by our Father.

> We all share this favored relational status—we are all beloved daughters of our Father in heaven.

A father's love is protective, unconditional, constant, and fierce. A father delights greatly in his daughter and has a special connection with her from day one of her life and throughout his lifetime. He always wants what's best for her, treats her tenderly, views her with eyes of constant favor, and is especially protective of her feminine frame. I see how my husband has a special connection with my daughter like this and it is delightful to me. Currently, three of my four boys have daughters and they are truly "smitten for life" with them! I so love seeing how they love their daughters in a special and unique way, not more than their sons by any means, but uniquely. As wonderful as this is, it's but a reflection of the much greater and perfect Father-love that God has for us!

Some of us have had fathers on earth who modeled this well, some not. We all have a mixed experience here since there are no perfect men (or women) on the planet. Whatever your starting point, it only gets better from the moment you invite Jesus into your life.

The process of facing the lies you have internalized about yourself and your heavenly Father from your life experiences is NOT easy. You have to be willing to feel to heal. You have to *own* your pain and brokenness before you can *disown* them.

I had a dad who truly loved me and gave me a great life. I honor him greatly. He was an amazing man who gave me much more than he ever had. He had many wonderful qualities that I am so grateful for. But he was wounded deeply by his childhood and never totally received the healing he needed, so in turn, he wounded those closest to him. Personally, I had father-pain to process when I met Jesus. That was the first place I went in relationship with God, to my wounded heart in this area. First came choosing to forgive each painful memory until every offense was buried in Jesus on the cross.

Next, I received prayerful, intentional, inner healing which helped me locate the lies I'd internalized about myself and God. By inviting Jesus, Immanuel (God with Us), into these places, I saw how He was with me all along, how He delighted in me, and I received the truth about who I am and who He is. I put off the lies and put on the truth, just as the Bible teaches us to do.

"Since you have heard about Jesus and have learned the truth that comes from him, throw off your old sinful nature and your former way of life, which is corrupted by lust and deception. Instead, let the Spirit renew your thoughts and attitudes. Put on your new nature, created to be like God—truly righteous and holy." Ephesians 4:21-24 NLT

I will include a template at the end of this book for Immanuel Journaling and Immanuel Healing Prayer, which I recommend as a very powerful way to engage with Jesus for the healing your heart needs.

Think back with me to the original vision I shared in chapter one. God initiated the process by first offering me a gift that was much better than I had. Here's how He did that with this foundational quality that He wanted to impart at the beginning of my Christian life:

A few months after being born again, I went to Europe as an exchange student for a year and lived in Luxembourg with a family there. As I was walking home from classes one day talking to Jesus as I went, I had an encounter that marked me. It was the Lord offering me one of those "grace-gifts" before I ever understood what I'm writing about now. I saw with my spiritual eyes huge arms wrapping around me, and I felt the loving embrace of the Father, which I'd never really experienced with my dad unless it was when I was too young to remember. It was tangible and powerful. It felt like sitting by a fireplace in a rocking chair on my dad's lap with His arms wrapped around me, very secure and safe, loved unconditionally and without limits, just because I'm His beloved daughter. I accepted this gift offer, and it led me to complete healing of my father-wounds over a period of years. I'm so thankful for it. It set the foundation for the rest of my life, rock solid and secure as His Beloved Daughter. I'm so thankful!

If this is what the Lord is focusing on with you, pray with me:

Lord, I am so honored to be your Beloved Daughter! I receive this revelation in full measure, and I welcome it. I pray for the grace to allow it to take over my entire being, to heal every part of me, to put off every lie, and put on the truth. I crawl up on your lap and open my heart to your Father-love now.

Mama Bear
Bearer of Mother-love

Mother-love is nurturing, constant, life-giving, lifelong, fierce, tender, tough, and unstoppable. It is the kind of love that comes from having been connected to your child in your own body. It's like the invisible, inseverable umbilical cord that endures for a lifetime after the physical cord is cut at birth.

> Mother-love is nurturing, constant, life-giving, lifelong, fierce, tender, tough, and unstoppable. It is the kind of love that comes from having been connected to your child in your own body. It's like the invisible, inseverable umbilical cord that endures for a lifetime after the physical cord is cut at birth.

Right now, my daughter Lisa is in the thick of motherhood! Baby number four in five years arrived not too long ago! At the moment, she and her husband and family are living with us after selling their home. Every day I'm getting the joy of witnessing her as a Mama Bear in action, tough and tender, deeply connected to her little ones, laying her life down for them. From my perspective, and Lisa's as well, there's nothing more meaningful, more delightful, or more difficult than motherhood. It's the primary cause of periodic lifelong insomnia! Even after babies start sleeping through the night, Mommas still lose sleep in other ways, no matter their stage of life. That umbilical cord tugs on you whenever there's a reason to be concerned for your child, no matter how old they are.

I love this quote penned by a well-known Christian author many years ago, still just as true today as it was then:

"You are as much serving God in looking after your own children, and training them up in God's fear, and minding the house, and making your household a church for God, as you would be if you had been called to lead an army to battle for the Lord of hosts." C.H. Spurgeon [12]

In Scripture, God is always referred to as our Father, but it is implied that He is also our Mother. He lovingly created us, birthed us, nurtured us, fed us, clothed us, looked after us, and has cared for us with painstaking detail throughout our lifetimes. He has protected us fiercely, even when we weren't aware of it. He has been tough and tender, depending on what we needed at the time (Hosea 11:3,4; Isaiah 42:14-16; Isaiah 49:15-18; Isaiah 66:13). If you are a mom, you know what I'm talking about!

If you aren't a mom, you can still understand that from your own heart and the ways you've experienced Mother-love from your own Mom or other women in your life. Women who have never had children are mothers in many ways as teachers, mentors, aunts, friends, caregivers, and more. There are no limits to the ways you can give and experience this kind of love; God's love in any of its forms is not restricted by any human limitations.

If you have had a mom who loved you in the ways I just described, it will give you a head start on "making the jump" to experiencing God's Mother-love in this way. Even if you've had the best mom in the world, there is always more of this that you will need, and you can get it as an impartation from God Himself. No human relationship will give you everything.

If you didn't have a mom who loved you like this, everything you need is available from God who is a Mama Bear as well as a Papa Bear! These are simply human roles by which we understand and experience the different facets of God's love.

I have a kind, thoughtful, loving mom and am grateful for her constant, consistent love. Her heart is always for me, always caring about my welfare. It has helped me make the jump to receiving God's love in this way. She has given so much to me, and I am truly grateful for her!

Even if you had the best mom in the whole world, she could never fill all the nooks and crannies of your heart that need mother-love. He intends to give this to you in all the places you have that void. He may use other women to be His carriers or just do it supernaturally—however He does it, it will be just what you need. There are many times I've experienced mother-love from other women and it hit the spot, really filled me up. Other times,

I had encounters with the Lord as my nurturer, caregiver, fierce Mama-Bear fighting for me, guarding my heart. I'm thankful for both!

If you feel the Lord is knocking on your heart, offering this grace-gift, open the door today. Release yourself into the loving arms of God as your "Mama Bear." Consider this:

"Even if my father and mother abandon me, the Lord will hold me close." Psalm 27:10 NLT

Lord, I want you to hold me close and fill me up with your Mother-love. I receive it today, and along with it, the grace to process any and every barrier in my life, to fill up every void I have, and to become to be a mature Mama Bear myself!

Precious Bride
The bearer of the gift of marriage

"Therefore a man shall leave his father and his mother and hold fast to his wife, and they shall become one flesh." Genesis 2:24 ESV

I never tire of the beauty and mystery of the union between a man and woman in marriage. I'm still in the afterglow of my youngest son's wedding. The look in Steve and his bride Rachel's eyes as they looked at one another during the entire wedding and reception was enough to melt my heart into a puddle on the floor! It was obvious from his loving gaze, the words that he said, and the songs that he sang that she was indeed "the one," his precious bride.

What a joy and a miracle it is that God brings two very different people together to make a covenant with Him and each other for life! I am truly grateful for this gift in my own life. My husband Michael has been such a treasure to me. We have learned through all the ups and downs of life to love each other well. For forty years now, he has been my faithful husband and best friend. We each know what the other one is thinking, feeling, and about to say before we say it. We have become intimate friends and partners in life. It's worth the work it takes to "become one flesh." In case you're wondering, it's not instantaneous; it takes lots of time and intentional effort, like most good things in life!

It also never ceases to amaze me that Jesus wants us, His people, as His bride! He wants us to be more than just obedient servants. He wants that marital kind of oneness with us too.

"For we are members of His body, of His flesh, and of His bones... This is a great mystery, but I speak concerning Christ and the church." Ephesians 5:30, 32 NKJV

From the time we are little girls, many of us dream of being a bride someday. That desire is in our hearts for a reason. We are made for this. We long to be "the beauty," the cause for that special man to leave his father and mother and commit to us for a lifetime.

> For some of us, we receive the gift of marriage on this earth. For all of us, we are the Lord's precious Bride, now and for eternity. There is grace needed for both! *With intimacy there is vulnerability, and with vulnerability, there is both joy and pain.*

I love this quote from Friedrich Nietzsche and thought it was worthy of note here:

"It is not a lack of love, but a lack of friendship that makes unhappy marriages."[13]

Perhaps a look at what true friendship means is warranted in our quest for happy marriages.

If you have a strong and happy marriage, you already know that no man can fulfill your desires and needs perfectly. We all need more than any human being can give us. So, whatever we lack on earth, God gives us Himself. That's what grace does.

But a happy marriage here on earth is not something all of us have. Some of us have difficult marriages, are divorced, or have never been or wanted to be married.

Wherever you stand today—married, unmarried, divorced—the Lord is here for you and wants to secure you in partnership with Him as His Precious Bride.

"The Lord will hold you in His hand for all to see–a splendid crown in the hand of God. Never again will you be called "The Forsaken City" or "The Desolate Land." Your new name will be "The City of God's Delight" (Hephzibah) and "The Bride of God" (Beulah), for the Lord delights in you and will claim you as his bride." Isaiah 62:3,4 NLT

Lord, I stand before you today and open my heart to receive this grace-gift. It amazes me that you want this with me. Come and take Your place in my life as my Bridegroom. Lead me into all the intimacy with you that I can possibly contain, and then give me more! I open myself up to receiving healing for all my wounds in every place my heart has been broken. I receive the new names you call me, "The City of God's Delight" (Hephzibah) and "The Bride of God" (Beulah). I receive You as the Love of my life, now and forever.

Soul Sister
Bearer of the gift of sisterhood

Sisters are born to love each other, to share a very special bond. We want to be there for one another, to be with one another, to work and play together, to share our wildest dreams, our greatest hopes, our deepest pains. We share this bond because of the family we are born into. For better or for worse, we are sisters for life. We are "blood" relatives.

Brothers are very special relationships as well, born to work and play together, share life and love together, to have each other's backs, motivate each other to be our best. For better or worse, we are brothers and sisters for life. We are "blood" relatives, too.

As sisters and brothers in Christ, we have that same special bond and we are also "blood" relatives, but it's the blood of Jesus that binds us together. Everywhere I go, especially when my husband and I minister in other churches around the world, when I meet brothers and sisters in Christ, there's an instant bond. In some cases, that bond can be closer than a brother or sister. When our natural sisters and brothers are born again, we may get to have that bond with them too.

Ladies, we all have a strong desire to share that kind of sisterhood. Groups of women can powerfully help each other, their husbands, children, and those in need when they build this kind of relational community, a real sisterhood. What would happen if we decided to put aside our differences, come out of our hiding places, make our lives "open books" with one another, to go to bat and to war for one another? Furthermore, what if we all committed to doing as much good together for this world as we possibly can in our lifetimes? I heard this quote recently at a women's retreat, and it struck such a deep chord in my heart. I want this to be my reality!

"If there ever comes a time when the women of the world come together purely and simply for the benefit of mankind, it will be a force such as the world has never known." Matthew Arnold, 19th c philosopher/poet [14]

Wow! That guy really "gets it"! He "gets us"! So how about it? Ladies—anyone want to do that?

If this is what the Lord is emphasizing to you, let this gift be yours today.

Lord, I come to you with the desire in my heart to have this impartation of sisterhood. I want to be the best sister I can be to my brothers and sisters, both natural ones and spiritual ones. Tear down anything in me that stands in the way, I pray. I want to have the kind of sisterhood that can bring people together centered on Jesus, simply for the benefit of mankind. May we become a force such as the world has never known!

Faithful Friend
Bearer of true friendship

True friendship is one of the greatest gifts this life gives us. It is a prize worth winning, whatever it takes. I love this quote by Thomas Aquinas:

"There is nothing on this earth more to be prized than true friendship." [15]

To have the kind of friends you want, you first need to be that friend to others! You will reap what you sow. How would you describe friendship? Here are some of the things I think about:

Friendship is always a two-way street. A friend is someone you find a connection with, share common ground with, one who gives you joy and who enjoys you, someone you delight in, and reciprocates that delight.

A friend takes the time to know your story—past, present, and future. A friend listens well and responds thoughtfully. A friend who stays in sync with you over time knows you so well that she or he knows how you're going to feel before you feel it, knows what you are going to say before you say it, knows you intimately, weaknesses and strengths alike, and still loves you. A friend loves at all times, even when she or he is weak. A friend respects you and serves you, and also is honest with you without judging you. A friend is there for you in times of need and loves sacrificially.

"A friend loves at all times and a brother is born for adversity." Proverbs 17:17 ESV

"Greater love has no one than this, that someone lay down his life for his friends." John 15:13 ESV

I remember hearing this saying as a little girl, "Make new friends and keep the old. One is silver and the other, gold." I believe it is true. Last night and today, I reconnected with two old high school friends, and this week, I will be with one of my college roommates. What a joy and a delight to rekindle those old friendships!

I treasure my friendships and make them a high priority. Going through life together is what friendship is all about. It's about connecting deeply and sharing hearts, laughing together, crying together, serving one another, studying the Bible together, and praying with and for each other. I miss my friends when I'm away because they are precious to me. We've done a lot of life together, the best of times and the worst of times. I care deeply about them. They hold my heart. They treasure me as I treasure them. I also enjoy the adventure of making new friends; you never know who might become someone special in your life if you open your heart to receive them as a friend. Relationships really are like silver and gold, the real "currency" of life.

> Make new friends and keep the old. One is silver and other is gold. Relationships really are like silver and gold, the real "currency" of life.

One thing about close friendship is that it is exclusive. Not everyone can be our best friend. We only have the capacity for a limited number of really close friends in our lifetime. Discernment is needed as we choose who we open our hearts to and who we make room for as a close friend. We can have many friends in a more casual way, but there needs to be a few select friends who can count on us and who we can count on too, no matter what.

"The man of too many friends (chosen indiscriminately) will be broken in pieces and come to ruin, but there is a (true, loving) friend who (is reliable and) sticks closer than a brother." Proverbs 18:24 AMP

As I mentioned before, relationships are the real currency of life. You are a wealthy person if you have true friends, and if you are a true friend, your friends are wealthy too.

To quote the movie *It's a Wonderful Life*, "Remember George: No man is a failure who has friends."[16]

We have all had relational disappointments in life, and we can end up being very guarded about friendships, always keeping a "safe" distance.

Never Unfriended: The Secret to Finding and Keeping Lasting Friendships by Lisa-Jo Baker[17] is a great read on this subject. She writes about friendships being based on trust. She explores how we can be trustworthy friends, choose trustworthy friends, and overcome those breaches of trust that broken or damaged relationships can cause. Her focus is on women's friendships—very insightful. It's on my recommended reading list for sure.

Once again, we acknowledge that there is no friendship on earth that "does it all" for us. Jesus Himself is that faithful friend that sticks closer than a brother, having laid down His life for us. He wants the friendship you have with Him to grow and deepen into the most intimate relationship you have now and forever.

So today, where do you stand in the area of friendship?

Lord, I want to allow You to shine your spotlight on my heart in this area. I receive the grace-gift of having You as my Faithful Friend, my best friend. I also want to get to the next level of being a faithful, trustworthy friend to my friends and to have those few faithful friends that go deep and last a lifetime. Let this seed of your grace for faithful friendship be planted deep in my heart today, growing up to produce a fruitful garden of friendship.

Chapter 1
THE VIRTUES
(part 3: Qualities of Nobility)

"As for the saints (godly people) who are in the land, they are the majestic and the noble and the excellent ones in whom is all my delight." Psalm 16:3 AMP

Merriam Webster definition: "The quality of being noble in character, quality or rank; the body of persons forming the noble class in a country or state. Synonyms: virtue, goodness, honor, honesty, decency, integrity, magnanimity, generosity, selflessness, bravery."[18]

> There are people on this planet that carry themselves with the dignity and quality of character that is reflective of true nobility. As Psalm 16 says, *"...they are the "majestic and noble and excellent ones in whom is all My delight."*

They may not hold any titles or ranks or socioeconomic status on earth, but they do in God's kingdom! There are some who do have these roles on earth as well as in heaven. There are some who hold such rank and titles on earth but do not at all possess the qualities of this true nobility.

I'm writing about the true nobility described in Psalm 16 in this chapter and those qualities carried by the angelic women who bore them.

Lady Pure Heart
Bearer of purity of heart

"Blessed (anticipating God's presence, spiritually mature) are the pure in heart (those with integrity, moral courage, and godly character), for they will see God." Matthew 5:8 AMP

"Who may ascend onto the mountain of the Lord? And who may stand in His holy place? He who has clean hands and a pure heart, who has not lifted up his soul to what is false, nor has sworn (oaths) deceitfully." Psalm 24:3,4 AMP

We know from other verses like Jeremiah 17:9-10 that the human heart is not naturally pure. Only God understands our hearts and can show us what needs purifying. Purity of heart is something you choose to cultivate like a garden. It's common knowledge that our hearts are prone to growing weeds that need to be pulled out regularly. In concert with the Master Gardener, we see where the weeds are and diligently uproot them.

Often, in my experience, circumstances in life and relationships will expose my heart. The Holy Spirit is an expert at laser-beam accurate discernment, helping me to see what God sees in my heart. I've already made the decision that I want a pure heart because I want to *see God* as He promises I will. Perfection is not required, just cooperation with the Holy Spirit. I am not under the law but grace, so I'm not the judge or the jury concerning myself and neither is anyone else. All I want to do is be like a child, easily led and pliable to the leading, guiding, discipline, and affection of the Holy Spirit.

I am not under the law but grace, so I'm not the judge or the jury concerning myself and neither is anyone else.

We all react to situations where the lack of purity in another person's heart is exposed. These days, when deceit and impurity are exposed, it's all over social media.

What about our own? It seems to me that judging others is a manifestation of our lack of purity of heart, what do you think?

What if we made a promise to ourselves to let others' hearts be God's responsibility and took full responsibility for our own? We would be on a faster track with fewer detours to "ascend the mountain of the Lord" and see Him clearly!

Consider this verse:

"The (intrinsically) good man produces what is good and honorable and moral out of the good treasure (stored) in his heart, and the (intrinsically) evil man produces what is wicked and depraved out of the evil (in his heart); for his mouth speaks from the overflow of his heart." Luke 6:45 AMP

The short version of this verse says, "Out of the abundance of the heart the mouth speaks."

A good way to become aware of what's in our hearts is to listen to our own words, listen with our "discerner" switched on—that is, when we are in tune with the Holy Spirit, we listen to those words and humbly respond to any correction that's needed.

Pulling weeds out of the garden of our hearts is about the willingness to admit when we don't have it right, to ask forgiveness of God and people when needed, receive God's forgiveness, and then change. We do actually need to *change* to get the weeds out. It has to go beyond words, to attitudes, and then to actions.

Consider this verse about how we can discern our hearts:

"For the word of God is living and active and sharper than any two-edged sword, and piercing as far as the division of joints and marrow, and able to judge the thoughts and intentions of the heart." Hebrews 4:12 NASB

The Word of God, written and spoken by the Holy Spirit, goes right down into your bones and shines the light on what's down there. I wonder if one side of the double edge represents thoughts, while the other side stands for intentions. At any rate, it can cut through from any direction it's being wielded and 'cut to the quick' right down to where truth can be seen. We need this sword to help us because we can't see clearly without it.

I had a dream one day about 14 years ago that gives insight into the kind of discernment we need, particularly with regard to our religious flesh. When we bought our current home, there was a tall plant with three tiers of leaves just to the left of the front step. I saw it every time I went through the front door and wondered, "Is that a garden plant or a weed?" One day, I came in the front door and just lay down on the couch for a quick afternoon nap. In the dream, I saw that plant and heard the Lord's voice say, "It's a weed. But it grows plentifully in my house because my people can't tell that it's a weed. He referred to the three tiers of leaves and what they represented. He said, "The first tier represents 'the pride of principled living,' the second, 'fear masquerading as wisdom,' and the third, 'selfish selflessness.'" Whoa. I felt the weight of that! I knew that this was the Word of God Himself speaking into the thoughts and intentions of my own heart.

"The pride of principled living" is what many of us do to get a sort of "code" working for us, so we don't have to humbly depend on God. Principles aren't bad. They are essentially good most of the time, but when they become a "code" we live by and take credit for, we can become quite proud of how good we are because we keep our code. It's a performance orientation that can sneak in and look good but not produce the kind of dependence on God that this Christian life is all about.

"Fear masquerading as wisdom" is pretty easy to see once you say it. Always erring on the side of caution may not be wisdom—it may be wise in many situations to take risks. It's again all about living in close relationship with God and not playing it safe, thinking that's always wisdom. The only safe place to be is in the middle of the will of God—and we need to know His heart and mind at any given moment about any given situation to know what wisdom looks like.

"Selfish selflessness" is a bit harder to understand. It took me a couple of months of interacting with the Lord about it to know what He meant by it. One manifestation that's more easily discerned is about doing things that "look selfless" but not having a heart of true selflessness behind it. It's something you have to ask yourself and discern for yourself with the help of the Holy Spirit. The other part of this is the tendency in religious flesh to denigrate the self—in other words, to constantly shame yourself and try to make yourself disappear because of the belief that the self is totally evil. The sinful nature is evil, but our true self was created in the image of God. It is really important not to "crucify" that self. Your original design is from God. It should be drawn out and reborn, bringing glory to God. You can do this by being your true self with Jesus in you.

These are my musings about purity of heart and how we can discern it. If that is something the Holy Spirit is impressing upon you now, open your heart and pray with me now:

Lord, today I want to make a promise to myself and You, to let others' hearts be solely your responsibility, and to be fully responsible for my own. I invite you, Holy Spirit, with your laser beam accurate discernment to search me and let anything you want to be seen come to light. I want to weed the garden of my heart. With Your help, I can have clean hands and a pure heart. To *see you* and know you are the greatest desires of my heart!

Divine Forgiveness
Bearer of forgiveness

"To err is human, to forgive, divine." Alexander Pope[19]

I wanted to include this with the virtues of nobility because it is probably one of the hardest and, therefore, most noble things we can do. It is truly impossible without God's help.

Here's what Wikipedia has to say about it: "Forgiveness is the intentional and voluntary process by which a victim undergoes a change in feelings and attitude regarding an offense. It lets go of negative emotions such as vengefulness with an increased ability to wish the offender well. Forgiveness is different from condoning (failing to see the action as wrong and in need of forgiveness), excusing (not holding the offender as responsible for the action), forgetting (removing awareness of the offense from consciousness), pardoning (granted for an acknowledged offense by a representative of society, such as a judge), and reconciliation (restoration of a relationship)."[20]

I think that's a pretty great definition of one of the supreme attributes of God. He forgave, He forgives, and He will continue to forgive us all. It's so true of Him that He took the judgment due to us upon Himself on the cross, died in our place, and rose again to show us how much He loves and forgives us. That's a forgiving God right there in plain sight.

"If we confess our sins, He is faithful and just to forgive us our sins and cleanse us from all unrighteousness." 1 John 1:9 ESV

"Bear with each other and forgive one another if any of you has a grievance against someone. Forgive as the Lord forgave you." Colossians 3:13 NIV

Sometimes forgiveness comes easily, but more often it doesn't—hence the reason for the 'seventy times seven' verse in Matthew.

"Then Peter came to Him and asked, "Lord, how many times will my brother sin against me and I forgive him and let it go? Up to seven times?" Jesus answered him, "I say to you, not up to seven times, but seventy times seven." Matthew 18:21,22 AMP

The way I have practiced this seventy-times-seven forgiveness is by simply silently praying. Whenever I have a resentful thought or feeling toward someone, I say, "I choose to forgive ____ for ___ today, I take it to the cross and leave it there where you reconciled all offenses. I receive your grace today and extend that grace to ____." I may have done that many times before, but I choose it again every time.

That is how I work through forgiveness. Every time I have a painful memory, a resentful or angry thought, anything at all that needs forgiving, I get it out in the open. After expressing it and how I feel about it, I surrender it. I just pray "Lord, I choose to forgive." Lots of times I don't feel it. I just choose to do it.

After many times of doing that with regard to my dad, I had an amazing experience. I was in a worship service with my husband, probably during the first year of our marriage. I engaged with God during the worship and was interrupted by a painful memory of something my dad had said or done. I simply prayed silently as it passed through my mind and emotions, "Lord I choose to forgive." Within a moment, I "saw" with the eyes of my spirit an enormous hand reach into my chest and pull out a big, hairy root. It really happened! It seemed like 'critical mass' had been reached, and I was from that moment on set free from a root of bitterness! After that root came out, I felt as clean as clean can be in my heart. I felt totally free to love my dad, and from that time forward, the scales were tipped. I was now living in the land of forgiveness, free of the root of bitterness that bound my heart. Practicing seventy-times-seven forgiveness freed me.

> After that root came out, I felt as clean as clean can be in my heart. I felt totally free to love my dad, and from that time forward, the scales were tipped. I was now living in the land of forgiveness, free of the root of bitterness that bound my heart. Practicing seventy-times-seven forgiveness freed me.

It seems that the Lord allows us to have "seventy-times-seven" people in our lives to give us the opportunity to practice this. In so doing, our hearts enlarge and we become more like God. We ourselves may be a "seventy-times-seven" person in someone else's life due to our own imperfections, so it's wise for us to extend mercy. We will receive mercy if we show mercy.

"Blessed are the merciful, for they will be shown mercy." Matthew 5:7 NIV

Another tool I've used to practice receiving and giving forgiveness is to draw a big block style cross on the front and back of a blank piece of paper. On one side, I write down my own sins that I was asking God to forgive me for inside the cross. On the other, I write down the sins and injustices that had been done to me inside that cross. Jesus died for the sins of the whole world, our own sins, and those who've sinned against us. The cross is the great equalizer where judgment and mercy meet. By doing this exercise, I get everything out of me and onto the cross in faith that the cross takes away the power of <u>all</u> sin. I experience the release of my own guilt as well as receiving justice for the injustices committed against me. All is rendered powerless in the cross. Then I rip up the paper and throw it away, or sometimes, I burn it if I happen to be around a campfire or somewhere I can burn it.

These kinds of symbolic acts of faith are powerful, like a ceremony that establishes a "stone of remembrance." When you do things like this, it establishes something so that, hopefully, you don't have to do it again. Just remember the work of the cross and the day you applied that work to your sins and the sins of others against you. This brings closure, it cleans out our hearts and minds and closes the door to thoughts that can torment us and weigh us down. Very powerful!

Lord, today I choose to forgive. I ask you to show me anything I need to be forgiven of. I also ask if there's anyone I'm holding hostage by not forgiving them and in so doing, holding captive myself by bitterness. I know I am not able to wave a wand and instantly make forgiveness happen. It is truly a work of your grace. I receive that grace-gift of Divine Forgiveness today.

Maid of Honor
Bearer of the gift of honor, being able to bestow honor on others

Honor is a most sought-after virtue, yet it seems harder to find in this current culture of ranting, unfiltered commentary and character bashing augmented by social media as well as TV.

I believe honor starts in our thoughts. If we think honorably, we will be able to show honor to others with the kind of respect, esteem, and affirmation they are worthy of. First and foremost, honoring God sets the context for honoring others who are made in His image. Honor makes its way from thought to speech to action. Honor requires that we protect our thoughts, guard our mouths, and be prudent about our behaviors.

> Honor makes its way from thought to speech to action. Honor requires that we protect our thoughts, guard our mouths, and be prudent about our behaviors.

"Finally, brothers, whatever is true, whatever is honorable, whatever is just, whatever is pure, whatever is lovely, whatever is commendable, if there is any excellence, if there is anything worthy of praise, think about these things."
Philippians 4:8 ESV

In our family, Michael and I have worked hard to create a "culture of honor." We intentionally instilled honor in each of our children. We insisted they find it in their hearts, their speech, and their behaviors to honor each other and others (and us as their parents, of course!) Today, they still honor us, each other, and others around them as well. It is a natural part of who we all are and how we do life together as a family.

We made a practice on every birthday, graduation, wedding, and other special occasions to come ready to speak affirmation and honor to the one being celebrated that day. I call it "love bombardment." They might call it something else or "just what we do" for one another. We celebrate each family member as worthy of great honor and respect, and we specifically speak it to each other on those occasions as often as we can. It's not just a blanket statement, like "you're awesome," but it's the specific attributes we see and respect in each other as individuals. I'm amazed at the beautiful things that come out of hearts as we are bent on honoring one another!

We are working to create this same culture of honor in the church we pastor now, New Hope Community. Small group settings are the best for making this happen, for setting a culture where people feel valued, respected, secure, and "called up" to be the best they can be.

In monarchies like Great Britain, honor is shown by kneeling, bowing, curtsying, bestowing honorable titles or awards—tangible acts that confer respect and recognition for honorable character and deeds. We do that in our culture by giving awards of recognition, not through physical postures and behaviors.

Today, I'd like you to use your imagination a little bit. Imagine Jesus kneeling before you. In His right hand, He is carrying His sword, the sword of the Spirit. The Father is standing behind Him sharing His thoughts about you. Jesus takes the sword and taps you on the left shoulder, then the right. He calls you by name and says, "You are mine, my beloved daughter, my precious bride, my dear friend. Here are the things I love about you." *(Listen to what He says to you. Let His thoughts pour into yours. Don't judge it, just receive it. Write it down, then repeat it out loud, and share it with others if you can.)* I honor you and bestow upon you, my Maid of Honor, the ability to carry yourself with dignity, to be free of shame, to think honorable thoughts, speak honorable words, and behave in honorable ways. Receive my honor for you today, and go, honor everyone else in your world in like manner."

Receive the honor today; let it permeate your being, let it dissolve all shame. Hold your head high and walk confidently. Honor those you love— husband, family, friends, people in roles of authority, and co-workers in your workplace. Honor those who are hard to love. Do not shame them. You are the Lord's handmaiden, bearer of His honor, conferring honor on others, creating a culture of honor wherever you are.

The Lord's Princess
Bearer of the gift of the royalty as a daughter

The daughter of the king and queen is a princess, right? It's her birthright, something she doesn't have to work for. She's born with it. She's royal. Likewise, because we are daughters of the King of Kings, we also have a birthright as the Lord's princesses.

> Being a princess is about knowing you are a favored daughter simply because you belong to Him. He looks at you with a sparkle in His eyes even when you are at your worst. There is nothing you can do to lose His favor. It's a status you own for a lifetime and beyond.

A princess doesn't carry the weight of the responsibilities of the kingdom. She simply enjoys the privileges of it and is invited to all the royal activities with other nobles in the king's courts. She is expected to conduct herself with "noblesse oblige," behaving in a manner worthy of nobility. But even when she doesn't behave herself, she is still who she is by birthright.

Ladies, that's who YOU are! By your birthright in the kingdom of God, when you were born again, you became the Lord's princess. Never mind if you didn't know how to behave yourself accordingly. You gained that status the minute you walked through that doorway from the kingdom of earth to the kingdom of heaven.

Princesses can get a pretty bad rap these days. There's a lot of mocking them. They are often portrayed as prideful, vain, useless weaklings. They are also portrayed as unhappy captives of a station in life that leaves them lonely, separated by wealth and titles from others they would like to have relationships with.

In spite of that, little girls tell a tale about all of us ladies whether we own it or not. Most every little girl I know has gone through a princess phase. My granddaughters are in it now. They love the tiaras, the long silky dresses with the big twirly skirts, being "the beauty," living in a castle, dreaming of dancing with a prince someday. They love the princess cartoons (and toys, backpacks, costumes, etc.). They love the stories of the noble ways in which princesses bring about change for the betterment of others by their virtue and strength. Princesses like Belle from *Beauty and the Beast*, Cinderella, Snow White, and more are that kind of royalty.

The truth is, we need to be a princess before we can become a queen. We need to be able to receive the secure status given to us as the daughters of the Most High King in our immaturity before we can move on to maturity.

Secure daughters move on into maturity without striving, without trying to earn or deserve. Being secure as a daughter of the One with the highest authority in the Kingdom is a prerequisite for stepping out with authority in a graceful, gracious way.

There are so many examples I can think of about women striving, grasping, demanding authority in ways that just aren't becoming at all. When we make choices to go after positions of authority or status without the security of knowing who our dad is and the innate authority we have, we will not carry ourselves with "noblesse oblige." We will use our strength to dominate others in destructive ways without that foundational security.

As women of God, we can be very strong, tough, capable, and able to speak our minds, letting our intentions and desires be known without stepping out of that secure place—that secure place of knowing who you are because of Whose you are is where GRACE abounds. When you stay in the place of grace, He will do far more for you because you trust Him. If you are insecure and feel like you've got to take matters into your own hands to make things happen, you usurp His place in your life. You will then hurt yourself and others in the process.

> That secure place of knowing who you are because of Whose you are is where GRACE abounds. When you stay in the place of grace, He will do far more for you because you trust Him.

"Cease striving and know that I AM God; I will be exalted among the nations, I will be exalted in the earth." Psalm 46:10 NASB

So today, if you are a woman striving to "find her place" and "make her way" in life somehow, would you consider first letting go and then finding that place of security as the King's daughter? Know who you are, the Lord's Princess, born royal with all the privilege and status you need. That need is already fulfilled. Come into your Daddy's courts and discover who you are because of Whose you are. Let Him be God. Ask your Father to do for you whatever it is you feel you need. He is able. If you let Him be Dad and you be the daughter, things will go well for you. Know your place; relax into it. Receive the grace-gift today of being the Lord's Princess.

Del Gratia, Regina (By the Grace of God, Queen)
Bearer of mature royalty as the partner of the King

This Latin phrase, Del Gratia, Regina, is found on coins from many countries such as the United Kingdom, Canada, Australia, and Sweden. In cultures that have a monarchy, it is believed that the role of Queen is a God-ordained role, one that God honors as He is honored in that role.

The queen is one who has that role by birthright or by marriage, the female monarch in a monarchy.

In the game of chess, the queen is the most powerful piece, able to move any number of spaces horizontally, vertically, or diagonally.

I'm an American. As an American, it can be difficult to relate to the way countries with monarchies treat royalty since we don't have that system in our country and current culture. As a society, we are fascinated with it and inquisitive about it. What is it that makes other cultures revere this position so? In Great Britain, the royal family does not have governmental authority, but they do have great influence and moral authority. In other countries, queens do have governmental authority which they may (or may not) exercise for the betterment of their people. In any kingdom, the queen has a sphere of great influence and authority, within her own kingdom as well as with other kingdoms.

We are the Bride of Christ, His Precious Bride to be exact, if you remember the previous virtue we explored. We are married to—made one with—the King of Kings and Lord of Lords. When we are mature enough, we can wield great power and influence when we are ourselves governed by the Holy Spirit. To have true dominion, we must be UNDER His dominion. If we love power, we become corrupted by it. If we love God above all, we can be powerfully used to influence and determine outcomes for good in our spheres.

> As a princess, we walk as a royal without all the responsibilities of royalty. As a queen, we are entrusted with responsibility for the Kingdom to use our authority for good, to accomplish the purposes of God on the earth, and to live out our divine callings to impact the world by our good works. There is much more at stake when you step up to be a queen.

The best example of this is Esther; her story is told in the book of Esther in the Bible. She was a favored daughter, who walked with great nobility of character as a young woman. Even though she was an orphan, she never seemed to feel sorry for herself. She trusted her uncle Mordecai, listened to his advice, kept her heart pure, and became a beautiful woman inside and out. She won the king's favor and found herself in the position of queen as a young woman. Her noble and gracious ways impressed many. And when an evil plot developed to destroy her people, the Jews, she spoke up. She enacted a very shrewd plan to expose the evildoer and save her people. She is still celebrated today in the Jewish culture for the honorable ways she lived her life as a Queen. She delivered her people, putting her life on the line to do so.

> Esther is a great picture of a favored daughter, who became a beautiful princess, who graduated to Regina Del Gratia by the grace of God and became a Queen. The Queen is a mature woman of God who is entrusted with great authority and responsibility on earth. She

| deeply loves and rightly fears God and genuinely cares about the people she serves. |

I think of how Esther navigated the existing social system in her husband Xerxes' kingdom, i.e. not able to even enter the king's presence uninvited (no ego problem there ☺). She knew her boundaries but had great faith. She knew how to use her influence to gain favor and took risks to open doors that were usually shut. She was like the Queen on the chessboard who could navigate in many directions without all the restrictions the king and other pieces had. She shrewdly and strategically carried out her plan. She wisely employed the prayerful intercession of her people and her uncle as she moved forward. She knew the power of prayer. It was clear that she knew she could die, but she decided it would be better for her to sacrifice her life so that others might live. She trusted God to be with her. And He was! She saw Haman hanged on his own gallows. Her people were spared as the reward for what she did as Queen.

We are all called to be Del Gratia Regina—a queen of the realm entrusted to us by God. We are called to mature as women of God, to know our authority and move forward in it, to do all the good He has intended for us in the time allotted to us. It is a sacred and solemn trust, a privilege and responsibility for each one of us. He wants us to be faithful to who we are and with what He has given us, not coveting what anyone else has. No one can do what you can do in your realm. If you don't step up to maturity, you won't complete that calling as a Queen in partnership with the King of Kings.

So today, will you take the step of faith, even though you may not be *there* yet in your maturity, to step up to the call to become Del Gratia Regina?

Lord, today, I receive this grace-gift of Del Gratia Regina, by the grace of God, a queen. It is intimidating. I am not sure I can do it, but something in me says, "Yes," today. I want to become that queen to do as much damage to the enemy's kingdom and as much good for the Kingdom of God on this planet as I possibly can in my lifetime. Let this grace-gift change me; transform me into an Esther, I pray.

Chapter 8
THE VIRTUES
(part 4: Character Strengths)

"We can rejoice, too, when we run into problems and trials, for we know that they help us develop endurance. And endurance develops strength of character, and character strengthens our confident hope of salvation." Romans 5:3,4 NLT

Fearlessly Courageous
Bearer of the gift of courage, boldness

The first example of a courageous, unintimidated person that comes to my mind is my son, Mike. As a little guy, he would boldly "go for it," whatever "it" was at the moment! Sometimes it was something risky, but he was not afraid. Even when a measure of fear would be a good idea! He is still not afraid of risk-taking today, and he has balanced out with wisdom that doesn't give way to fear. It has helped him keep on moving forward in life without being paralyzed by the fears that plague so many. Because of this, he brings great encouragement to those around him. Courageous people en*courage* others!

I can think of lots of women who are really courageous. There are some whose children have made poor choices, yet these women have found the courage to love them well and bear them forward while their hearts are breaking and bleeding. Some women have illnesses, physical or emotional pain they live with, and they still choose to be actively serving others, praying, maintaining an outward, other-centered focus. Others have taken risks to increase the quality of their lives, families, and careers. Some have left behind financial security to be free of a life-draining situation and seek the life they were born to live. Others have stepped up to the plate in positions of authority to make this world a better place, making personal sacrifices for the benefit of others. I know their names and see their faces as I write this. They are everyday heroes, unintimidated by the challenges that have come their way, making courageous choices daily. Sure, they wrestle with fear, but they press through it and find the courage to keep on living and loving.

Think of the famous women you know from history or ones you admire today. People like Anne Sullivan and Helen Keller, Joan of Arc, Anne Frank, Harriet Tubman, Mother Teresa, Marie Curie, Rosa Parks, Benazir Bhutto, Amelia Earhart, Margaret Thatcher, Condoleezza Rice, and many, many more. The Bible is full of courageous women like Esther, Mary, Jael… who would be on your list?

But you don't have to be a famous person to be famous in heaven. Courage is a rare and powerful quality that many women exhibit in their everyday lives.

I often marvel at the courage of Mary, the mother of Jesus. She was 14 when the angel came to her to announce His plan to make her the mother of His child. Can you imagine that at 14 years old? (Or at any age for that matter?) That's truly an intimidating prospect for any woman! Even though it is an amazing honor, wouldn't you be at least *somewhat* terrified? She was engaged to Joseph, and this would make life very complicated for their relationship. She had no idea what the future would hold with this kind of responsibility—all the unknowns would have been very scary.

> Very often the things that scare us to death are the very
> things that make us into the courageous people we
> are destined to be. They either make us or break us.
> *Courage isn't the absence of fear; it's choosing to move*
> *forward anyway, shaking in your boots!* C. S. Lewis says,
> *"Hardship often prepares an ordinary person for an*
> *extraordinary destiny."[21]* Yes, I agree, it takes courage
> to make it through the hardship. But for the sake of an
> extraordinary destiny, it's worth it, wouldn't you agree?

Think of the times when you said "no" instantly to something or someone and later regretted it because it would have been an amazing opportunity. You were afraid you didn't have what it took or were afraid to leave the security of the known for the unknown, non-secure future, pregnant with possibility. Think of the times you had to face really difficult, painful realities and felt your knees buckle and your fearlessness melt like butter. You wanted to give up, but something in you rose to that occasion. Something said, "No, I will not be afraid! In faith, I'm choosing to take courage."

> Your lioness heart coupled with the Holy Spirit calls to
> you from deep within your soul, pulling you to your feet
> to be the best you can be!

"For God did not give us a spirit of timidity or cowardice or fear, but (He has given us a spirit) of power and of love and of sound judgment and personal discipline (abilities that result in a calm, well-balanced mind and self-control)." 2 Timothy 1:7 AMP

That's what I'm talking about! It's a supernatural thing. The Bible says, "Fear not" a total of 365 times! Amazing, that's one for every day of the year. Let the reader understand that it's likely we will experience some kind of temptation to fear every single day! Therefore, the grace of God, His supernatural provision of the Holy Spirit in us, is here to help us live a *fearlessly courageous life* in spite of ourselves.

What a powerful gift!

Is this the grace-gift you most need today? We need it every day for sure, but there are seasons when we see the strongholds of fear in ourselves overpowering us. We realize that we need to "bust" those strongholds to establish a life characterized more by courage than fearfulness.

So, Lord, I receive this gift today—I want to be a Fearlessly Courageous woman. Let courage explode within me and make me a lioness-hearted woman! Thank you for giving me the grace I need to overcome every fear and every fearful pattern in my life. I welcome it now, in Jesus' name.

Personality Plus
Bearer of the gift of being authentically, totally yourself

"For you formed my inward parts; you knitted me together in my mother's womb. I praise you, for I am fearfully and wonderfully made. Wonderful are your works; my soul knows it very well. My frame was not hidden from you, when I was being made in secret, intricately woven in the depths of the earth. Your eyes saw my unformed substance; in your book were written, every one of them, the days that were formed for me, when as yet there were none of them." Psalm 139:14-16 ESV

> All of us are as unique as snowflakes. Not one of us is the same, though we may share common characteristics. When God made each one of us, He used a special recipe. He then kept the recipe but created a new one for the next person. Only God knows the intricacies of our "frame," but we intuitively live out of that original recipe, which I call our "original design."

But life happens. Sometimes we never fully discover who we were born to be, never quite discover those ingredients we were made with. Sometimes we do discover at least a measure of our original design, but we get buried in the cares, worries, busyness, and pains of life. We forget who we are. We believe lies about who we are, who God is, and about the way life works.

Since the fall of man, we have regularly gotten sidetracked. We have to find our way "home," back to our original design and purpose, minus the sinful nature we also inherited. Jesus dealt a deathblow to that sinful nature and installed His own in us. Jesus within us helps us shed that old part of us as we journey toward discovery of who the Father originally intended us to be. The vision described in chapter one depicts the process of putting off the old and putting on the new, renovating our lives as we do so (See Ephesians 4:22-24).

If you never really know who you were born to be, you will never really know why you're here on the planet. Understanding your identity and purpose is foundational to being your full self and finding your true destiny.

Growing up, my dad would take me with him to farms he managed around the state of Ohio to take soil samples. Before planting crops each year, he would go around to all these farms, obtain samples, and do soil testing. These tests would determine which elements were present in that soil already and which fertilizers would need to be added. When I was in grade school, he bought me a soil testing kit. It was a small chemistry set that I would use to test soil samples to see what specific nutrients were in that soil (e.g., nitrogen, magnesium, calcium, phosphorous, etc.). Drops of certain chemicals would change the color in the soil test tube to reveal what the soil contained or what it lacked. The process and what it revealed fascinated me. Thankfully, it wasn't my little test results that determined what Dad would use to fertilize the soil on his farms! He had professional soil testers to determine that.

Our personalities are made up of various elements; our "soil" is strong in some areas and weak in others. We aren't supposed to have all the elements in our personalities. Our strengths and weaknesses are hard-wired in us on purpose. We just get to discover what those purposes are! It's like solving a mystery or putting a puzzle together. Our different personalities are all meant to fit together into a grand plan—the Master's Plan—for purposes greater than ourselves.

There is NO SHAME in having weaknesses. Perfection is not what makes us lovable, acceptable, likable, or presentable. It's the imperfections in a work of art that make it a masterpiece. None of us are made up of weaknesses alone. We have amazing strengths as well.

That brings me to the "Plus" part of the name of this quality: Personality Plus. I think Jesus puts the plus in our personalities. When His personality lives inside of ours, the two bond and blend. Like two best friends or a married couple, we begin to think alike, act alike in some ways, feel with and for one another, still separate and distinct, but our thoughts, feelings, actions start to harmonize. We become more of who we truly are when He's within us. Our personality is sanctified graciously by that partnership. Amazingly, He compensates us for our weaknesses. That's what grace does—it compensates.

In addition to pastoring alongside my husband (http://radius-group.org) I am a professional life coach, founder of Fully Alive Coaching, LLC (http://www.fullyalive5.com). I'm a trained and certified ICF coach (http://www.coachfederation.org) and I'm a master coach with Dan Miller's 48 Days lineup of coaches (http://www.48days.com/coaching/). Using the DISC test as a basis, Dan has developed a Personality Profile test I use, like a soil test, to help determine the particular elements of your personality. It's simple, like a snapshot, not a super detailed test like some out there. That's why I like it.

If you'd like to check out this test to see some of the ingredients in your personal "recipe" of personality traits, you can go to my coaching website and purchase the Personality Profile. After you take the test, the results will come directly to you in your email inbox. Have fun with it!

Lord, today I know I want to go deeper in understanding my original design. I feel like I need to return "home," to rediscover my identity and purpose, to get crystal clear on it. And I want to do more and more harmonizing with you in me. I want that Personality Plus gift today! I receive it and with it the grace for all the compensation and sanctification you want to give me. I want to be fully me with Jesus in me!

Total Security
Bearer of the gift of security

When a person is secure, you can see and feel it. They know who they are, have accepted who they are, they like themselves, and are at peace with their weaknesses. They are confident, less ruffled by what others say or think about them, and less apt to be knocked off course in life.

Here's the truth about us women, a quote from Beth Moore's book *So Long Insecurity: You've Been a Bad Friend to Us*:

"Every woman is insecure about something, her looks, her relationships, her career, you name it. The problem is, not only does insecurity make us miserable, it cripples us and makes us feel worthless. But no woman is ever worthless-especially in the eyes of God."[22]

Isn't that the truth?

Men and women alike are prone to insecurity with some differences in the way it plays out for men versus women.

> When a person is secure, you can see and feel it. They know who they are, have accepted who they are, they like themselves and are at peace with their weaknesses. They are confident, less ruffled by what others say or think about them, and less apt to be knocked off course in life.

As I'm writing today, I'm thinking, "Who is one of the most secure people I know?" Instantly a young, twenty-year-old man, the son of one of my dearest friends, came to mind. His name is Joe Schuchardt. Joe was born early, halfway through my friend Terri's pregnancy. He was extremely premature, about 3.5 pounds, I think. He was in the NICU for a month or more, fighting for his life. His lungs kept collapsing, but he survived with the help of life support *and lots* of prayer. My husband Michael was one of the people visiting him in the hospital in Miami where Joe was being cared for. It was a touch-and-go situation. Everyone there and back home in Kansas City was praying intensely for him. Miraculously, he lived. He made it, but he had permanent damage to his brain: cerebral palsy.

Joe has always been in a wheelchair, has never walked without assistance, still talks with difficulty, etc. But Joe is one of the most *incredibly secure* young men you will ever meet! During his senior year of high school, he was honored by his classmates, teachers, and school administrators alike for his incredibly positive attitude, hard work ethic, and for his encouragement to others. I was there when he spoke at the senior class assembly and brought the house down! He loves Jesus with all his heart, is known for his passionate faith, and he's a prayer warrior. Joe doesn't seem to be bothered much by his special needs. He is simply so secure in himself and in the love of God that it doesn't matter. He totally believes he will be healed someday. I do, too. When I was so very ill, Joe would often come to the prayer meetings my friends held for me. His prayers were instrumental in my healing! I hope my prayers will be instrumental in his healing. I truly believe he will walk someday. Even if he doesn't, he will do more good on this earth than many people who have every body part in nearly perfect working order. Why? Because he is so full of faith in God and so very secure in himself.

Joe's parents, Bob and Terri, had a big role in showing him the kind of love he needed to feel secure in himself and in relationship with them. They made sure He was introduced to God's love from a very young age. But in the end, every person must make a choice themselves to move forward into maturity in relationship with God and to find their ultimate security in His love. Joe made that choice early on in life, and he is such a shining example for others to see.

That's what I'm talking about—that's total security! It's personal security, i.e. having accepted yourself, liking yourself, being at peace within yourself and with your strengths and weaknesses. Add to that finding secure relationships with family and friends. Combine that with being secure in God, knowing you are fully accepted, delighted in, and loved by God—then you have TOTAL SECURITY—that's the total package deal.

What would you say about yourself? Are you a secure person in your self-acceptance, in your relationships, and in the love of God?

Lord, I open my heart to you. What do you see? I choose today to receive the grace-gift of Total Security from you. Let it go to work on my insecurities today. They are not serving me, You, or anyone else. I let them go and receive, in full, the security you want to form in me. I want the "total package deal."

Graceful Dancer
Bearer of the gift of grace, graciousness

When I had the encounter described in chapter one, the *dance* was front and center in my life, a dominant theme. I believe it is a metaphor for GRACE. Biblically speaking, grace means a couple of things. I've heard these taught in church for years:

1. The freely given, unmerited favor and love of God.
2. The influence or spirit of God operating in humans to regenerate or strengthen them.

The big thing about grace is that it is FREE, absolutely free. Free of charge, free of the need for merit, free of deserving, free for the asking. It just needs to be received. Another thing about grace is that it's given on an "as-needed" basis. In other words, you get it when you need it. It's not something you can store up in the pantry for later use; it's hot off the grill when you need it most.

Growing in grace is about growing in your capacity to live with the consciousness of your need for grace and your ability to quickly and easily receive it. It's a dance. You can get good at it, learn the steps, stay with your partner, and recover quickly from missteps. As you improve, you release all sense of needing to earn or deserve and melt into the strength of God to lead you.

> When we mature in grace, we become graceful, gracious women.

In my early 30's, I went through a time when the Lord was emphasizing grace in my life. He wanted me to understand it and "live in it" at a new level. The tendency is to welcome grace at the doorway of salvation, then kiss it goodbye when you're "in the house"–as if the outworking of your salvation is something you do by your own efforts. It doesn't take too long to realize that this doesn't work. You fall flat on your face and "run out of gas."

I was taking a walk all alone one day and wrestling with the Lord about something I couldn't release and couldn't find the grace for. I had run out of gas. In the midst of my conversation with Him about this, He said, "Here's how my grace works."

I immediately saw a picture of a long stairway with many, many (way too many!) steps to the top. I saw myself looking upward and thinking, "I'm too tired to go all the way up there, I don't have the strength, and it will take too long." Then the Lord said, "All I am asking you to do is put your foot on the first step." So, I did that. I knew what that first step was concerning the issue I was wrestling with, and I did it. I prayed a simple prayer to forgive and release someone. Immediately, the stairway became an escalator! I was suddenly at the top without any effort other than taking the step I was asked to. Amazing. He said, "That's how grace works. You do just the part I'm asking you to, nothing more, nothing less. It will take all you have just to do that step. But when you do, I will take it from there, all the rest of the way." I've never forgotten this. It was a turning point for me in my understanding and experience of grace. It's a habit now to take that first step, then "take the escalator!"

I think of the parable of the loaves and fishes in the Bible (Matthew 14). Of course, the Lord knew there wasn't enough food available for 5,000 people! He wanted to show His disciples how His grace works. All He required was what they had available. There were two fish and five loaves. Perfect! He simply took what they offered and made it work, and miraculously, amazingly, 5,000 people had lunch that day in the middle of nowhere!

The truth is, all any of us ever really have in this life is a couple of fish and a few loaves! Compared to the limitless power and resources of God, that's all we've got. All that He requires is for us to offer up what we have in hand, openhearted, open-handed, not holding back. He will take what we offer Him and multiply it beyond our wildest imaginations.

"Are you tired? Worn out? Burned out on religion? Come to me. Get away with me, and you'll recover your life. I'll show you how to take a real rest. Walk with me and work with me—watch how I do it. Learn the unforced rhythms of grace. I won't lay anything heavy or ill-fitting on you. Keep company with me, and you'll learn to live freely and lightly." Matt 11:28-30 MSG

Lord, today I come and offer what I have in hand to you. I come needing grace, knowing that I need it. Receive my offering and multiply it like the loaves and fishes. Deliver me from the struggle to make things work with my limited strength. Let your grace fill me, making me graceful and gracious, like a GRACEFUL DANCER.

Timeless Beauty
Bearer of beauty, inside and out

Beauty is pleasurable to the senses and stunning to the mind and soul. It's one of the qualities people seek for most in this life—beauty of all kinds. When you see the beauty of nature, you feel a sense of awe and wonder. It restores your soul, draws you into its sweet, intoxicating fragrance. Beauty for women, especially, is such a core desire. I spoke about this earlier in the section on The Divine Invitation. We were born to be beautiful inside and out. We know that, we pursue that, we pay for that!

Outward beauty for women comes in all kinds of packages, many different skin colors, hair colors, fragrances, fashions, shapes, sizes, ways of walking, talking, and carrying ourselves. We all want to look our best in any and every season of life. It's an innate part of who we are. It shows that we care about the beauty we've been given, it's a good thing! Taking care of your physical appearance is like wrapping a gift with the appropriate wrapping paper. What's inside is the genuine gift of value. How it's presented is very important, and it enhances the delivery and reception of the gift. Presentation matters!

Inward beauty is about having the qualities I'm talking about in this book, virtues of character and personality forged in relationship with God and other people. This kind of beauty is timeless. It is a now-and-forever beauty. *It matters MOST!*

Without the beautiful things in life, we would find it difficult to process the ugliness of life. When it's up to us, we do well to fill our lives with beauty of all kinds. Beauty in family and friendships, in our surroundings, taking time to be in nature, doing beautiful things for others, filling our minds with beautiful thoughts, sights, sounds, smells—all of these things matter. They fill us up with wonder, with the awareness of God. He is absolutely beautiful. He made us beautiful too.

"Finally, brothers and sisters, whatever is true, whatever is noble, whatever is right, whatever is pure, whatever is lovely, whatever is admirable, if anything is excellent or praiseworthy, think about such things." Philippians 4:8 NIV

Both the beauty in us and what we see in nature are only reflections of the beauty of God. We can easily be incredibly 'wowed' by that beauty, but it's only a fraction of His. Consider this:

"For ever since the creation of the world, His invisible attributes, His eternal power and divine nature, have been clearly seen, being understood through His workmanship (all His creation, the wonderful things that He has made), so that they (who fail to believe and trust in Him) are without excuse and without defense" Romans 1:20 AMP

"Worship the Lord in the beauty of holiness!..." Psalm 96: NKJV

We need to know that we are beautiful in God's eyes no matter what. Your child is always beautiful to you even when they aren't doing well or looking so good. You're never ugly to Him. Sin is ugly, but you aren't, and He's working all the time to clean the mud off of you to reveal the true and beautiful person He made you to be. He is working in you to reveal the beauty inside you. He's like a Master Potter. We are all "clay pots," and He chose that material to form you into the beauty He had in mind when He created you.

"But we have this treasure in jars of clay to show that this all-surpassing power is from God and not from us." 2 Corinthians 4:7 NIV

As long as I can remember, I've heard the phrase, "Beauty is as beauty does." Here's what I want to convey about that. First, we need to "be the beauty," then we can "do the beauty" without it becoming a performance trap.

Step up to "BE" the beauty; step out to "DO" the beauty.

Being the beauty has to do with owning who you are, seeing yourself as a beautiful treasure in a jar of clay that God greatly values. Accept His value of you. Believe it. Receive it. Abolish all lies you may carry inside you that say you aren't beautiful. Resolve the issues and complaints you have about your physical appearance, do what you can to change them, and accept what you can't. Let your countenance reflect what God sees in His eyes. He looks at you with great delight! You are His delight, day and night.

I'll tell you a story about a struggle I have had in recent years that might help you. When I went through my health crisis with trigeminal neuralgia and had brain surgery to stop the seizures, I suffered from a side effect of the surgery caused by swelling in my brain. The left side of my face was paralyzed. I woke up from surgery still in a lot of pain but without the seizures, thank God, but my face had been rearranged! At first, I was in so much shock about all that had happened to me that I barely paid attention. I think I also thought maybe it would go away.

It didn't go away, and one day it hit me. Hard. I only had half a smile. I couldn't drink from a cup without it dripping all over because half my mouth wasn't working. One eye was now smaller than the other. I no longer felt the same sense of beauty I had felt before; I was now scarred.

I battled the lies that I wasn't beautiful anymore, that having half a smile meant I could only have half the joy now that this had happened to me, that I must've done something wrong to deserve this. I struggled with feeling that my grandchildren would cringe as they looked at all the photos taken with me from now on, and they would be ashamed of me. None of that stuff was true. Nonetheless, I had to wrestle with it, come to Jesus with it, and internalize what He said was true about me. That always trumps the pathetic lies the devil peddles.

In the section on Gratefulness, I described the practice of Interactive Gratitude—expressing gratitude to God and then listening to His response. I do this in prayer and also in journaling. Even though I was struggling to find anything to be thankful for, I decided to practice gratitude regarding my crooked smile and rearranged face. Here's the journal entry I wrote. I titled it "My Wisdom Smile."

My Wisdom Smile

Me: "I'm realizing that a measure of the discomfort I still feel about my facial palsy is due to focusing on what I've lost rather than what I've gained. In so doing, the loss becomes magnified because whatever I choose to focus on becomes magnified in my eyes. So, I'm choosing to focus now on what I've gained through facial paralysis:

1.) I'm grateful that this surgery did relieve the seizures and some of the pain.
2.) I'm grateful that I can relate to many more people who have suffered loss of any kind. I have much more empathy and compassion.
3.) I'm grateful that I am still beautiful even with my crooked smile, and the radiance of internal beauty does not diminish with age or physical imperfections.
4.) I'm grateful that people feel loved by me when they see their reflection in the sparkle of my eye, not the perfect shape of my smile.
5.) I'm grateful for the intrigue that may be created by my crooked smile—I'm naming it my "wisdom smile." It lets others know that I have a story to tell about what I've gained from suffering, loss, and overcoming something painfully difficult. It invites others to do the same and gives them hope for their lives.

Jesus replied: "I couldn't have said it better myself!"

I really like this saying about scars from Carly Simon: "*A really strong woman accepts the war she went through and is ennobled by her scars.*"[23]

Actually, I believe that our scars make us more beautiful. Whether physical or internal, they tell a story of battle and victory but not without cost. An overcomer is more beautiful than someone who has not yet been tested. Perhaps she is twice as beautiful!

The thing is, love makes us beautiful. The fact that we are deeply, eternally, and unconditionally loved makes us beautiful. When we know we are loved, we can truly love others. And we become more and more lovely as we learn to love well.

My grandkids don't care at all if I have a crooked smile. They care if I love them! That's what makes me beautiful to them. That's what makes us all most beautiful. I think maybe that's where the word "lovely" came from!

Lord, I receive the gift of Timeless Beauty. Beauty is in the eye of the beholder, they say. I look into Your eyes to see the beauty You see in me. Plant it deep in me—and let me "BE" the beauty. Then let me move out of that "BEING" to "DO" the beauty. Let me reflect Your beauty to all the world around me. Let me love well and become more and more lovely with every passing day.

Grateful (On her back was written Appreciated)
Bearer of the gift of gratitude

My grandson Graham is one of the most grateful little people I know! He is three years old. He says, "thank you," for just about everything. He will stop in the middle of a conversation and say "thank you" for something that crosses his mind. It is truly a lovely trait in him! I appreciate that about him and desire to be like him when I grow up! He has made a habit of being grateful at the age of three. That's what happens when we choose to be habitually grateful; we reap what we sow. When we are consistently grateful, we will then be appreciated. That's exactly how it works.

I define gratitude simply as a felt sense of wonder, thankfulness, and appreciation for life.

Bible scholars, scientists, sociologists, counselors, and experts across the board from many disciplines have done years of studies. Consistently they've found that gratitude is one of the most powerful things a person can have to improve their well-being and quality of life. That's without a relationship with Jesus, so how much more are these things true for those who do! What these scholars have found is simply a confirmation of what the Bible teaches. Gratitude to God opens us up to connection with Him, and all good things come from Him.

> *"Enter His gates with thanksgiving; go into his courts with praise. Give thanks to him and praise his name." Psalm 100:4*

When we give thanks to Him, He opens His gates to us—to come into His presence and to connect with Him. So, gratitude is essentially "the password into His Presence."

> *"Be thankful in all circumstances, for this is God's will for you who belong to Christ Jesus." 1 Thessalonians 5:18 NLT*

When we stop in the middle of a difficult circumstance and choose to be thankful to God, instantly we open up our awareness to His presence. Yes, something uncomfortable or painful is happening, but He has never left you. Immanuel is with you! When you are aware that He is with you, you can experience His peace, His Shalom. You are not alone. All is well with your soul.

When you give thanks to God, pause and listen for His response to your prayer. You can then receive whatever He expresses to you and become even MORE engaged with Him. I described this in the section on Peaceful Tranquility. Gratitude is like a "reset" for our souls, pushing away the stress and anxiety and bringing us into peace in His presence.

I will include some instructions for practicing Interactive Gratitude at the end of this book. I highly recommend it as a regular practice in your life. It has been transformative for everyone I know who does it.

Years ago, the Lord said this to me: *"Whatever you choose to focus on will be magnified in your eyes."*

> *Whatever you choose to focus on will be magnified in your eyes.* If we focus on the Lord with gratitude, He will be magnified in our eyes. And He is always "bigger than life," bigger than we can ever imagine

When He spoke that to me, He also gave me this picture. I saw myself sitting on a couch with a large magnifying glass in my hand. First, I was looking down at the floor through it, and what I saw was dirt, dust, bugs, and debris. They were magnified, bigger than life, and making me feel agitated. Then I lay back on the couch and lifted the magnifying glass upward toward the sky. Suddenly the Lord's face filled it and overtook the whole scene. I was suddenly undone in His presence, flooded with awe and wonder. All was well with my soul. All I could do was say "Thank you!" And this verse came to mind:

"Oh magnify the Lord with me, and let us exalt His name together! I sought the Lord, and he answered me and delivered me from all my fears." Psalm 34:3 ESV

If we focus on Him with gratitude, He will be magnified in our eyes. And He is always "bigger than life," bigger than we can ever imagine.

Lord, I want to be a more thankful person. Let it become my default response in all circumstances, as well as something I intentionally choose to do as my way of life. I believe that if I am thankful, I will also be appreciated. I want that for sure! I receive the grace-gift named GRATEFUL today. Thank you for offering it to me! (Jesus responds: You're welcome!)

JOB'S SISTER
Bearer of the gift of being tried by fire, emerging "better, not bitter."

In my 30's and 40's, I committed to read through the entire Bible in a year. Those were my busiest years of raising five children, but I made it a priority for several years.

The first few years I read through the entire book of Job on the annual schedule. It was depressing. I didn't understand exactly what was making him have such long arguments with God and other people. I didn't understand why God actually said "yes" when the devil asked permission to test him. I was more like Pollyanna than Job, a born optimist. It didn't fit well with my bent.

So, I decided to read only the first and last chapters of Job, chapters 1 and 42, and then be done with it for the year ☺ (confession is good for the soul).

Then in 2004, I began to live my own Job story. All of a sudden, my world was turned upside-down when I was hit with the trigeminal neuralgia, aka the "suicide disease," a seizure disorder of the 5th cranial nerve. After about two months of living in excruciating pain, I finally got the correct but sobering diagnosis. I went to Mayo Clinic in Jacksonville, FL to have a brain surgery to stop the seizures. I'll never forget the morning I went in for that surgery. An African man stood holding the door of the operating room open. I looked in the room and saw the "saw" that would be used on my skull. I shot him an anxious look and he smiled back at me and said, "Welcome to the land of miracles."

The miracle of the surgery that day was that the seizures stopped, thank God! However, I still had severe, searing pain in my face because the nerve was demyelinated, which means that the coating was disintegrated so it was like a "live wire." Also, the left side of my face was paralyzed, I saw double, and my hearing was impaired on the left side. I needed a cane to walk, a patch on my left eye and a plug in my left ear. My life had suddenly become like a waking nightmare.

After being discharged from the hospital a week later, my husband and I went to stay with an old college friend and his wife there in Jacksonville who just so happened to be the head of the Jacksonville Mayo Clinic. They graciously opened their home to us while I recovered. On the first night, I lay in bed in complete shock. My mind was spinning. I thought, "Surely this is all just a bad dream! I'll wake up, and it will be all over." I stilled my mind and began to pray. I said silently, "Lord, what on Earth are you doing? What is going on here?" I sensed His presence in the room, and He replied, "This is about you and me becoming the best of friends." I was speechless. I thought, "This is really not the way I would go about that!" Then I clearly sensed *His loneliness*. I prayed silently, "Lord, you *have so* many friends, how can you be lonely?" He went on to say, "I have a lot of friends, but not many who are the best of friends because when I take them through this kind of trial, they don't want to be my friends anymore." I thought, "I get that!" But I also realized just how serious He was. Then He said, "You'll never know all of me until you know me in the fellowship of my sufferings. Through suffering, you come to know parts of me that you hadn't known before, like Job did." Wow. I fell silent for a while. Then I responded. I said, "Well, Lord, if that's what this is about, I'm in. Just let me end up where Job did in chapter 42."

The next two years were full of pain, being incapacitated on the couch, not being able to sleep, not being able to take care of my two high school boys still at home. I had to be on pain meds, I could not eat much because of facial pain, and the list of physical sufferings was endless. At the same time, the church we had been a part of for 20 years went through a severe testing with lots of fallout. My husband was one of the pastors. At that same time, my father-in-law, who lived with us at the time, went through a terrible health crisis as well. My husband had three traumatic situations to deal with simultaneously, and my own heart was in as much pain as my body sometimes.

I had one of my most profound experiences of the love of God I'd ever had during that time on the couch. I was in such severe pain that my whole body was trembling. I cried out to the Lord to help me, and He showed up. Suddenly I felt a tunnel of wind all around my body and inside me. It felt like I was being lifted up off the couch. There was a message in that wind, a revelation from God. In it, He was saying, "I cherish you, I cherish you." That message went with that wind throughout my entire being. I couldn't do one thing to merit that. I believe it removed a residue of performance orientation in my life. I received His intimate, cherishing love that day and never lost it. In a new way, I understood what intimate fellowship with God was, right in the middle of the most intense suffering. His love transcends ALL circumstances!

During that time, I got more honest with God than ever, and the book of Job became my manual! When any human being is tested to that degree, it is inevitable that the kind of questions and arguments Job had will surface. When a person has to endure so much pain and suffering, all those thoughts and emotions boil to the surface and spill over in the midst of the fiery trial. Now I understand that.

I also understood in a new way that all my sufferings are His sufferings. He was feeling all of it with me, bearing it all with me. I thought back often to the experience I'd had with the Lord at Sacre Coeur, knowing that He had been preparing me then for what I was experiencing now. It's so easy to feel like God has abandoned us when we go through intense times of suffering. Jesus felt that on the cross and cried out, *"My God my God, why have you forsaken me?" (Matthew 27:46 NIV)* when He reached the end of His human capacity to bear it all.

In the same way the Lord clued me in ahead of time at Sacre Coeur, He also did with Jesus. The cry of Jesus on the cross in Matthew 27:46 was foretold in Psalm 22:1,2 in the time of King David! Jesus as a Jewish boy would have learned those verses in Psalm 22. When he cried out those exact words on the cross, He was expressing the depths of human emotion but also the recognition that what He was experiencing was foretold. He had been prepared. He was actually not alone even though He felt like it. His Father had given Him those words long ago as a lifeline to hold onto when He needed it most.

Why does God do this? He knows we will reach the end of our capacity to cope with the pain we are experiencing at those times in life when suffering hits most intensely. So, He lets us know somehow ahead of time, with the hope that we will be prepared and know that He is with us when we feel He must have abandoned us. What I now know is that He wants you to know beyond a shadow of a doubt that He is ALWAYS with you, no matter where you are, rain or shine, light or darkness. Romans 8:31-39 sums it up, culminating in this verse:

"…neither height not depth, not anything else in all creation, will be able to separate us from the love of God that is in Christ Jesus our Lord." Romans 8:39 NIV

During my season on the couch, I got really mad at God one day. I had reached a breaking point. I just couldn't hold it in any more. I went into the garage, got into my car, locked the doors (as if that made a difference) and yelled at Him! I shouted, "Why did you say "yes" to this? Why did you let this happen to me?" I just let it all out for several minutes, expressing exactly how I felt. Afterward, I felt very sheepish. I came back into the house and laid on the couch apologizing for what I'd just done. A moment later, I simply saw with the eyes of my spirit His smiling face, beaming at me. He said, "You can never lose my favor, not even on your worst day." I melted in a puddle of tears. The anger subsided. I felt peace. I felt loved. I simply needed to get that all out. Much to my amazement, it was okay with Him.

There was a transforming work of grace done in my life during that time. I now realize that some of the ingredients lacking in my natural humanity were added to me in the flames of this fire. As I said, my natural personality tended to be more like Pollyanna, an eternal optimist, a natural encourager. I still have those traits, tempered now by a keen awareness of the darker hues of truth about life. I am still a naturally positive, encouraging person, but much more empathetic with the sufferings of others and the consequences of life in a fallen world. I just "get it" more and have capacity for all of life. Pollyanna and Job are now friends. ☺

More than ever I am confident and unshakeable in knowing that God is with us at ALL times in ALL things EVERYWHERE. Absolutely nothing can ever separate us from His love!

There were so many blessings that came to me at that time in my relationship with Him and from people who came to pray for me and serve my family. I saw the Lord in a whole new way, and we did become the best of friends. I was fully healed of the pain, the double vision, the hearing impairment, and was finally able to get off the couch and do life again. I still have some facial palsy, but today I am strong and healthy, older and wiser, and very thankful for every day of life I get to live. And I did end up where Job did in chapter 42.

"… I know that you can do all things and that no purpose of yours can be thwarted… I had heard of you with the hearing of my ear, but now my eye sees you." Job 42:2,5 ESV

I repented of how small I had made Him to be before that time, how my limited understanding of His plans put Him in a box. I realized that truth is both dark and light as Psalm 139 says. He had introduced me to the darker hues of truth. Most importantly, He was with me all the way.

> We will never know all of Him until we know Him in the fellowship of His sufferings, and *all of our sufferings are His sufferings*. He cares deeply about each and every one of His children. We can be the best of friends if we embrace Him and find him in the darkness as well as in the light.

Don't become offended with God or anyone He might use to be a part of that suffering. Let it all go, forgive, trust Him, and become better, not bitter. This is what happened to me. I now have much more trust and depth of relationship with God, more empathy and compassion for the sufferings of others, more understanding of grieving and how to walk through it into a new reality.

God is good *all the time*. Life isn't always good. But He is, and He loves you.

Lord, I want to be the best of friends with you. I want to know *all* of you and to receive this grace-gift that will make me better not bitter, to be JOB'S SISTER. Take my hand now and walk with me. I TRUST YOU.

Unsinkable Hope
Bearer of the "hope that does not disappoint"
(Romans 5:5)

Hope is simply a strong and confident expectation of good things to come. It is like a lifeline that drops down from heaven and invites us to grab it, hold on tightly, and let it carry us upward. I picture it like a hot air balloon in the sky, defying gravity, inflated with the breath of God. Hope floats.

When I was in college, I had an opportunity to attend an Urbana Missions Conference in Urbana, Illinois. One of the main speakers there was Corrie Ten Boom. For those of you who may not know of her, she was a Dutch Christian woman who had been captured along with all of her family by the Nazis in World War II and imprisoned in a concentration camp. Her family harbored Jews in their home to hide them from the Nazis. When they were discovered, they were all sent to the concentration camp where her whole family died except for her. She wrote a book called *The Hiding Place*[24] which tells the whole story, from which a movie was made.

At that time, Corrie was an elderly lady with gray hair, support hose, and orthotic shoes. She looked every bit like a Dutch grandma! I was a 21-year-old Jesus person in ragged bell-bottom jeans with long, straight, blond hair, a child of the 70's. But that day, when I heard her speak, she became my sister, a spiritual Mother from afar, a kindred spirit to me. Corrie told her story of the atrocities she had seen and lived through, the hardest of which was the death of her entire family in the concentration camp. She shared how the Lord came to her when she was no longer able to take it anymore, when her heart was overwhelmed, and she was at the point of giving up. She said many people around her died from their hearts just giving up, they lost the will to live. She quoted Romans 5:5, saying this was her favorite verse:

"...and hope does not disappoint because the love of God has been poured out within our hearts through the Holy Spirit who was given to us." Romans 5:5 NASB

At her very lowest point, the Holy Spirit came upon her and flooded her heart with the experience of His love. She felt overwhelmingly, unconditionally loved, and was lifted up from that low, low place to the heights of His living, loving Presence. That was, she said, how she made it out of that awful, evil place alive. She emerged from there and went around the world telling her story and inviting people to come to Jesus. She had an amazing life and ministry. She never married; she just loved the Lord and served Him wholeheartedly to the very end of her days.

I was riveted as she spoke, not even sure why I was so drawn to her and her message. When I was in the midst of my very own "Job" story, her words from 30 years ago came back to me. Truthfully, it came to me many times before then when hard times came, and I was tempted to lose hope. Romans 5:5 is now my favorite verse too.

I've come to understand that hope is the anchor for faith and love. If we lose hope, we lose heart, and we give in to despair.

"Three things will last forever–faith, hope, and love–and the greatest of these is love." 1 Corinthians 13:13 NLT

"Therefore we do not lose heart. Though outwardly we are wasting away, yet inwardly we are being renewed day by day." 2 Corinthians 4:16 NIV

Once, when I was struggling with losing hope over a situation, I got this picture from the Lord: I saw a baseball diamond. First base was labeled Hope, second base was labeled Faith, third base was labeled Love. I was aware that the strategy of the enemy was to take us out at first base so that we would never make it to second or third. I was also aware that this was the reason that Hope was the most assaulted of the three. In this world, disappointment comes easily, and it would be the ground where the enemy would try to do His dirtiest work. The goal was to cause us to *lose heart* as Corrie was tempted to in the concentration camp.

I think of Sarah, who hoped in God, not perfectly, but, ultimately, she did. When she felt like she couldn't take it anymore, she made a poor choice and took matters into her own hands. The result was not what she had hoped for! Her heart was weakened by grief and disappointment, as evidenced by her pained laugh when the angel came to promise that the baby she had hoped for would be born one year from that time. Then, when that happened, she truly, joyfully laughed as her hope was fulfilled at the birth of Isaac! She went down in the Hebrews 11 "Hall of Faith" (Hebrews 11:11, 12). Even though she hoped and believed imperfectly, she is one of the heroes of faith.

"Hope deferred makes the heart sick, but a longing fulfilled is a tree of life."
Proverbs 13:12 NIV

> When our hearts are overwhelmed, God comes to us with that Romans 5:5 love outpouring in our hearts, He compensates us with that love. He gives us the hope that does not disappoint, that isn't anchored in OUTCOMES. It's simply anchored in the ocean of His love. That is the deepest longing of our heart fulfilled.

There's a reason HOPE has always been symbolized by an anchor. I used to have a charm bracelet with an anchor, a cross, and a heart—hope, faith, and love. Hope anchors the other two. Faith and love spring from an undying hope that has been rightly placed in the love of God.

I believe that by the grace of God, it is entirely possible for us to choose to be unsinkable, refuse to be deflated, and to maintain a strong and confident expectation of good things to come.

Lord, I open my heart today to receive that Romans 5:5 love outpouring that will anchor my heart in the right place, that grace-gift of UNSINKABLE HOPE.

Passionate Sage
Bearer of the gift of wisdom and passion combined

At the beginning of the year, around New Year's Day, I always spend time waiting on the Lord, asking about the new year and what He has to say about it. The word I got about 2017 was: "Wisdom and passion together in equal proportions simultaneously."

In my thinking, that translates to becoming a PASSIONATE SAGE. I think it was another confirmation to me that this was the time to write my book. It was that season in my life.

A *sage* is a "wise one," one who has simplified understanding to what's most essential, sifting and sorting what to throw away and what to keep. It's keeping the best and most profound truths, synthesizing them, and throwing the leftovers, the nonessentials, away. It's boiling it all down to what's most important in life. *Knowledge expands, wisdom simplifies.*

Here's something the Lord said to me as I was doing Immanuel Journaling one day recently:

> "Wisdom comes from syncing with Me as you metabolize and synthesize beauty and pain."

Please make this statement a callout in the middle of the text right where it occurs

Wow—that has exploded inside of me.

Staying relationally connected to God while digesting and processing the beauties and joys of life along with the pains and sorrows of life is how we get wisdom. That's it—that's really how it happens!

Something else the Lord dropped on me one day was this phrase:

> "Knowledge expands, wisdom simplifies."

Please make this statement a callout in the middle of the text right where it occurs

Don't we live, now more than ever, in a world that believes more knowledge is better? The exponential growth of knowledge is astonishing and exhausting! It seems to me that the knowledge of good and evil is increasing at such a rapid pace we can't keep up with it. I don't think we were made to keep up with it. In the Bible, the tree of life is very different from the tree of the knowledge of good and evil. We simply aren't built to know so much! Only God can pull that off. Our finite brains are going haywire with it all.

Knowledge can be very helpful when used in service to humanity, such as the amazing developments in medical science that help cure diseases. I'm not "dogging" all that expansive increase of knowledge.

But it does seem to me that there is an acute shortage of *wisdom*. Wisdom simplifies and synthesizes, comes up with what is most valuable, honorable, loving, and virtuous. It doesn't "kill" passion when doing so.

This can only come from staying relationally connected to the Lord, learning to sync up with the "mind of Christ" which is within us.

"For, who can know the Lord's thoughts? Who knows enough to instruct him? But we understand these things, for we have the mind of Christ." 1 Corinthians 2:16 NLT

We can never know it all. If we ever think we do, we become a "know-it-all"! That's not 'becoming' in the least. But we know someone *who does* know it all. He can share His thoughts with us on a "need-to-know" basis. I'm so very thankful for that!

Throughout this book, I've emphasized that *it's not about religion; it's about relationship*. If we disconnect relationally from Him, all that's left is religion. We are left to our own devices, and we try to figure things out on our own. Not a good plan.

Without staying in relationship with God, we can become overly cautious and fearful about everything in reaction to the pains of life. Lots of times this kind of caution and fearful living can masquerade as wisdom. Fear masquerading as wisdom doesn't qualify as real wisdom. Always erring on the side of caution isn't real wisdom. It shuts down the heart and the passion that fuels our hearts. It cools us down instead of firing us up.

Real wisdom engages the heart and engages relationally with God and people. Real wisdom is *passionate*. It stays *fired up* about life, about loving people, doing new things, and taking calculated risks. Wisdom is about living life fully alive!

"Wisdom is the principal thing; Therefore, get wisdom. And in all your getting, get understanding. Exalt her, and she will promote you; She will bring you honor when you embrace her. She will place on your head an ornament of grace; A crown of glory she will deliver to you." Proverbs 4:7-9 NKJV

My son Luke has what I would call an *innate* gift of wisdom. It's like he was born 80 years old or something! I marveled at the insights that would come out of his little-boy mouth. No one told him the things he seemed to "just know." He has had plenty of trials and tests in his life, but he still keeps the most important things the most important things. He reminds me of what's important when I talk with him. And he has managed to keep himself passionate as well. He is a good example of a person who has passionate wisdom.

Wisdom is there for the taking if we want to have it. Jesus Himself is wisdom personified. So, what do you say?

Lord, today I open my heart up to receive wisdom and passion combined in equal measures simultaneously. I want real wisdom, the kind that engages my heart passionately, wisely, stays fired up, and pursues living life fully alive. I receive today the grace-gift of the PASSIONATE SAGE.

Chapter 9
THE FINALE - FULLY ALIVE

Let's take a moment and go back to chapter one and re-read the account of this woman:

"After they had all given their gifts, they stepped aside. A hush filled the room followed by a sense of anticipation. One last woman came into the room. Her presence filled the entire place. Her countenance was so bright that she lit up the whole atmosphere around her. She was a bit intimidating because of the power and authority she carried. But the most powerful thing about her was the love she exuded. Her name was 'FULLY ALIVE.' She was fully alive in Jesus and He in her. She was standing tall, laughing out loud, and crushing a serpent's head under her feet.

> She was fully alive in Jesus and He in her. She was standing tall, laughing out loud, and crushing a serpent's head under her feet.

"She was the *composite* of all the others, a woman who was truly a great soul, an overcomer, able to fully live and give from the abundance within her. She was the epitome of Christ formed in a woman who was fully herself. She was "redeemed Eve" who had finally crushed the serpent's head under her feet (Gen. 3:15). As I pondered this analogy of Eve, I realized that it was the serpent's THINKING (which is in his head) that she had overcome, the very same poisonous thinking he had injected into her mind in the Garden of Eden. Jesus began to reverse the effects of that poison that exists in Eve's daughters when He died on the cross. He took the poison upon Himself and mysteriously became the antidote. When we receive Him, we also receive the 'antivenin' (antidote), which makes the reversal of the serpent's thinking in us possible. The woman named 'Fully Alive' symbolized the promise of complete recovery and redemption. She overcame and stood in a new place of dominion, by His grace and her determination to believe the truth in every part of her soul."

She was the 'pièce de résistance,' i.e. the most important, outstanding part of this entire encounter.

She was the total of all the others that went before. When all the virtues had been imparted and integrated into this woman, in the midst of processing all the beauty and pain of life, she became the epitome of Christ formed in a woman who was fully herself. To be Fully Alive is to be fully you with Christ fully formed in you. That's a bit of a mouthful, but I think that about sums it up. This is "redeemed Eve." Every time I remember this, it still takes my breath away.

Take a deep breath now and close your eyes. Visualize YOURSELF as that woman. Put your face in the picture I've just described. There's so much light beaming from your countenance that you brighten up the entire atmosphere around you. Because of the power and fearlessness in you, you are a bit intimidating. The most powerful things about you are the LOVE you exude along with the authority you carry. You have your head thrown back laughing out loud, standing tall, crushing a serpent under your feet. You are an overcomer, a truly great soul, able to fully live and give from the abundance within you. You have learned the dance of liberation unto transformation to the rhythm of grace with your partner, Jesus. You have stepped up to BE the beauty and are stepping out to DO the beauty. You have shunned religion and embraced relationship. You are an OVERCOMER by the virtues of the godly life you have chosen to live. You have crushed the serpent's thinking under your feet and live in harmony with the mind of Christ within you. You are wise and discerning, capable and compassionate. You LOVE WELL because you know you are well-loved. YOU ARE FULLY ALIVE!

Breathtaking, isn't it? I believe that is YOUR promise from God—that He is making you THAT woman. This is where you are headed.

> There's something about visualizing this for yourself that engages your faith. It becomes a pending reality rather than a distant possibility.

"Faith shows the reality of what we hope for; it is the evidence of things we cannot see." Hebrews 11:1 NLT

When Elijah prayed for rain, it first showed up as "a cloud the size of a man's hand" in 1 Kings 18. Then it grew and became a torrential rain quenching the terrible drought in the land. When you SEE something, you begin to move towards it in faith, which engages you in the process of it coming to pass. God does His part, and we do ours.

Faith is about seeing the unseen and living from the unseen. Who we become as we do that will one day become SEEN-KNOWN-REALITY!

I am thrilled to know that this is the destiny He's offering all of us, His beautiful daughters, His fully alive women, if we dare to hope and believe it!

"The glory of God is man (and woman!) fully alive." St. Iranaeus, 2nd c. AD

Lord, I dare to believe this today! Help me to keep this picture you've shown me of my destiny always before me let it be my focal point, my lifeline of faith moving me steadily forward toward the realization of it. Help me do the dance with you.

I accept this Divine Invitation!

In your journal, I'd like you to write the date, then your name and this statement of faith. "Today, I, _____, see myself as FULLY ALIVE." Then describe in detail what you visualized, how you saw yourself fully alive. I encourage you to think of that image as often as possible, even find a way to create a picture of that however you might choose. When I shared this vision with women in our church, the husband of one of them had a painting commissioned of her face as the Fully Alive Woman. She kept it on her wall to remind her every time she walked by it. Another woman created a devotional using all of the women and their virtues of the Fully Alive Woman, adding images for each one. Find your way to "own" this and make it your own!

Becoming Fully Alive doesn't mean we somehow magically only experience the good things in life. *It's about being able to synchronize with Jesus as you metabolize and synthesize both the beauty and the pain.* Life will bring us lots of both of these. Living life fully alive means that you keep your heart open and vulnerable rather than hard or unfeeling. It takes major courage to live this way. Embracing both joy and sorrow with an open heart takes a lot of courage and a lot of capacity relationally. You have to be able to hang with God and with people and not shut down. *This is what it means to be fully alive.* There's no way it can happen apart from living in continuous, open communion with God. This 'Divine Invitation' is about the kind of relationship with God that leads to the ability to keep on loving well.

There's a song that captured my heart years ago that I'd like you to listen to when you have time. It still makes me tear up every time I hear it. My youngest son, a worship pastor in Siloam Springs, AR, dedicated it to me in his church on Mother's Day this year and sent me a video. It really touches me how Steve knows my heart! He is truly one of the most sensitive, thoughtful men I know. Steve is like a young David, a psalmist, a pastor, and a man who lives from his heart. I received the video of Steve performing the song as I was writing this chapter, and wanted to include the lyrics, but they are quite long. So I will ask you to check it out with whatever you use to listen to music. The lyrics are available using a Google search. A well-known version was done by singer LeeAnn Womack. Many others have done renditions since. It's called "I Hope You Dance."[25]

Basically the song is musing about life, the ups and downs of it all. We regularly get to choose whether we will stay engaged and 'dance', or sit down and resign ourselves to a mediocre or unhappy existence. It's easy to sit on the sidelines rather than dance bravely on the stage of life! This song calls to all of us to continue to make the choice to *dance* no matter what life brings us. With Jesus as our dance partner, how can we *not*??? My prayer for you is that no matter how many times you get knocked down or miss a step, you will always choose to get back up and get back in the dance! Jesus is waiting for you on the dance floor, extending His hand every time.

The divine invitation awaits your rsvp 24/7.

Welcome to the dance of becoming Fully Alive!

Chapter 10
WHERE ARE YOU NOW?

First of all, I want to give an invitation to any of you who may not know Jesus yet, anyone who hasn't experienced what I described in chapter two when I was born again. The Lord Jesus is with you wherever you are, ready to receive you when you come to him in faith and surrender. He loves you dearly! If you have a friend who knows Jesus, it would be great to have him or her pray with you. If not, this miracle can happen with just you and Jesus right here, right now.

In this section, I share a "pathway" to help you take those steps of faith that lead to becoming born again. My husband Michael created this based on *The Lord's Prayer*. Think of each phrase of *The Lord's Prayer* as a "stepping stone" of moving toward Him, acknowledging the truth of each one. Engage in prayer with Him. End with accepting the gift of salvation by believing in your heart and confessing with your mouth that Jesus is your Lord. Receive Him in your heart by trusting him with your entire life—past, present and future. Give your all to the one who has given His all for you. If you know someone who is a Christian, get in touch and maybe pray with them or connect with them after. Go with them to church and get involved in a healthy community of Jesus' followers where you can grow and find that Fully Alive life I'm talking about! Let me know if you make this commitment—you can contact me via the contact forms in one of the websites listed in the "About the Author" section at the back of the book. Welcome, welcome, welcome to the kingdom of God!

How to Begin Your Personal Relationship with God

Your heavenly Father, your Creator, is truly willing and eager to connect with you heart to heart. He wants you to be His, and He wants to be yours. He is your heart's true home. Like any relationship, it's a two-way street. However, long ago, God accomplished His part to lay the foundation for this personal friendship with you. He is the one who has initiated this relationship and the Holy Spirit has already been at work to draw you to himself and to His son, Jesus Christ.

When His first followers asked Jesus to teach them to connect with and talk to God, He shared a special prayer with them that provided them with simple and profound things to say to him. This prayer is known as *The Lord's Prayer* and it still works today!

Get into a quiet space, all alone or with a trusted friend or two who have already met Jesus, and then, in your heart of hearts, relax and welcome God's presence to come near to you. Take your time… this is about your relationship with the living God! It deserves your attention and focus. First, read through the prayer found in Matthew 6:9-13 (Good News Translation).

Our Father in heaven,

May your name be honored,

May your kingdom come,

May your will be done,

As in heaven, so on earth.

Give us today the bread we need now;

And forgive us the things we owe, As we too have forgiven what was owed to us.

Don't bring us into the great trial, But rescue us from evil.

You are the rightful ruler of heaven and earth,

Your power is supreme,

You alone deserve the highest praise.

Next, mediate on each phrase of the above prayer and consider the thoughts in parentheses to help clarify what you are praying about.

- *Our Father in heaven* (Your Creator lives in an invisible dimension nearby that interfaces with our visible world. He wants to be to you what a truly good Father is, no matter how broken, or strong, your relationship with your earthly father has been.)
- *May your name be honored* (The *name* points to the *nature* of God that has been demeaned and mocked by us in the past and by so many people in our world. Feel sorry for this, as you are able. We want this to change in the days ahead.)
- *May your kingdom come, May your will be done, As in heaven, so on earth.* (Ask now that the presence, ways, and purposes of the Holy Spirit will sweep into your life and that people in our world will experience the peace, joy, wisdom, and love that are fully known and shared in highest heaven.)
- *Give us today the bread we need now* (God longs for you to *trust him*, each day and every hour, for all the practical things you need to sustain your life. Apologize to him for any ways you've been trying to make your life work in your own strength. He is a generous Provider and wants to be honored in this way.)

- *And forgive us the things we owe* (In this, you are asking for forgiveness for all your sins and failures. This is possible because Jesus went to the cross and shed His blood as a "sacrifice lamb" and died. He died for us all; He died for you. He faced and triumphed over all the evils, of all the ages, and of all humanity by dying on the cross. His resurrection from the dead on the third day confirmed the fact that evil and death were vanquished. Thank God for His forgiveness of all of your sins.)

- *As we too have forgiven what was owed to us.* (Make space in your heart for the free gift of God's forgiveness in Jesus by *letting go of all* unforgiveness, resentment, and bitterness toward anyone who has wronged you. Also, release any *blame* toward our good God for allowing bad things to occur in your past. These are toxins in your heart that will gradually destroy your life if they are not released to God. You are invited every day to bring all the pains of your life to the cross of Christ and place all injustices, large and small, into His capable hands. This doesn't mean that what happened to you was right or okay. It also does not mean that you must have a trusted relationship with an abusive person. It simply means that you have put these matters into God's hands so you can be free to enjoy His love, peace, and joy.)

- *Don't bring us into the great trial* (Ask God to protect you and lead you away from engaging in situations that are outside the boundaries He sets for you. Ask Him to keep you from trying to make life work in your own wisdom or strength.)

- *But rescue us from evil* (Evil is real and there is a very real invisible adversary, the devil, who is seeking to assault and deceive you and the people around you. He tempts, lures, entices, lies, and manipulates people and situations and attempts to sabotage your friendship with your heavenly Father, His Son, and His Spirit. Do not fear but simply ask God to equip you with wisdom, strength, and power for this battle and to be your Captain in the spiritual battle between good and evil. It's a good fight!)

- *You are the rightful ruler of heaven and earth, Your power is supreme, You alone deserve the highest praise.* (You are closing your prayer with a good confession by which: 1) you gladly acknowledge Jesus as the rightful Lord of your life; 2) you recognize that His power is greater than all other powers, both visible and invisible; 3) you have rejected all other "gods" (idols) and will reserve your deepest affections and highest compliments for who He is and what He has done.)

Feel free to go back through this prayer again and again until it becomes more relational and warm. It's the prayer Jesus Himself taught us to use. Thank Him now for listening to your prayers—He has heard you and is glad that you trust Him. May He be with you now and always!

The Secrets of Spiritual Growth

*"...but let your adorning be **the hidden person of the heart** with the imperishable beauty of a gentle and quiet spirit, which in God's sight is very precious." 1 Peter 3:4 ESV*

When we talk about encountering God, we are talking about engaging Him with "the hidden person of the heart" described in the verse above. This is our "inner sanctum," our "holy place" of communion with God. He created us for daily communion with Him in this place. Every day, my husband and I begin our day with a devotional called *Jesus Calling* by Sarah Young and we pray together. Then we do our separate Bible studies alone or with other people. We have our own prayer times, journaling times, and we share what the Lord shows us regularly. As we cultivate this relationship with God in "the hidden person of our hearts," the fruit of that spills over into all of life and into our entire beings. The hidden person of the heart has senses, parallel to our physical senses. The Bible is full of references to this:

"And you shall love the Lord your God with all your heart and with all your soul and with all your mind and with all your strength." Mark 12:30 ESV

"Watch over your heart with all diligence, for from it flow the springs of life."
Proverbs 4:23 AMP

"Oh, taste and see that the Lord is good!" Psalms 34:8 ESV

"Call to me and I will answer you, and will tell you great and hidden things that
you have not known." Jeremiah 33:3 ESV

"So give Your servant an understanding mind and a hearing heart (with which) to
judge Your people, so that I may discern between good and evil." 1 Kings 3:9 AMP

"I pray that the eyes of your heart may be enlightened…" Ephesians 1:18 NIV

"…your anointing oils are fragrant; your name is like ointment poured out…"
Song of Solomon 1:3 ESV

Sometimes we encounter Him in the "aha" moments of reading and understanding Scripture, other times in prayer when we intuitively "just know" something. We may get a picture in our minds or see a picture of something we are looking at suddenly take on a new meaning. There are times we are undone because of the powerful, tangible presence of God. We may hear His voice speaking clear words to us or have more subtle impressions. There are multiple ways He communicates with us, but communicate He will! That's what relationships are all about, a two-way communication between two people who care about each other.

Because this hidden person of the heart is hidden, we have to intentionally seek out, access, and develop these capacities. We must make it a priority for our spiritual development. As I write this, our daughter and son-in-law and their family are living with us, and they have a 4-month-old baby. For that baby to develop, he requires time, verbal and visual engagement, touch, feeding, resting, and basic needs met. He needs an environment that enables him to thrive. In the same way, we develop our inner being by attuning ourselves to the Holy Spirit living within us, joined to the hidden person of the heart. Consider this verse:

*"But when you pray, go into your **most private room**, close the door and pray to your Father who is in secret, and **your Father who is in secret**, and your Father who sees (what is done) in secret will reward you." Matthew 6:6 AMP*

I love this verse! I believe our "most private room" can be more than one thing. It is a special private place we go for prayer, and I also think of it as the "hidden person of the heart" (*1 Peter 3:4*). I see our "Father who is in secret" as the indwelling presence of God. You take that private room with you, with Him in it, wherever you go. In order to cultivate that relationship, solitude is required, a "prayer closet," where you can give focused, undivided attention to God. If you live a life of devotion to God, of pulling away from everything daily to commune with Him so as to develop your spiritual life, then it will spill over into all the rest of your life. It will never be easy, but you will be blessed if you choose to live this way.

I married a pastor and God blessed us with five wonderful children. Life was extremely busy and demanding, especially when they were all young! That made it even more important for me to cultivate a life with God that was strong, deep, and overflowing in all of life. Some days, I didn't feel much overflow, but I always had an intentional, daily quiet time (usually during the hour when my little ones were watching Sesame Street ☺). It's like making deposits in your bank account so that you have a surplus to draw upon when the inevitable withdrawals come. Because I did this, there were many benefits in life that came to me. It enabled me to encounter God in the midst of the chaos because I had encountered Him in my "secret place."

I want to encourage you to position yourself to encounter God on a regular basis. Expect it. Get in a quiet environment with worship music on in the background, pray and listen, look, engage with your senses. If it's not familiar for you, just practice being in the presence of God and journaling what you believe you are hearing, seeing, tasting, smelling, and touching. Let your entire being engage with God. He is there, always. He wants you to know Him better than you know any human being on the planet. Make it your usual way of life to study Scripture, alone and with other people. For years, I read through the One Year Bible, now I do more intensive study of specific books of the Bible. Also, throughout the years, I've gathered in a home with friends or in a church to do Beth Moore Bible Studies, or a Priscilla Schirer study, or a good Christian book of some kind. (I'm hoping this book will also be one that women will use to do this kind of study!)

I would also recommend doing a book study of *Living From The Unseen: Reflections From a Transformed Life* by Wendy Backlund. In this book, she helps guide you through both teaching and experiential exercises to encounter God as a normal part of life.

I believe God made us to be supernaturally natural beings, or naturally supernatural beings, whichever way you want to say it! It is my hope and prayer for you that this will become a "new normal" for you if it isn't already.

The Immanuel Life

The word Immanuel means "God with us." All that I've been describing in this book is to lead us more and more into knowing and experiencing "God with us" to the point where it is the "new normal" for us to live in the continual awareness of God's presence. I love the story of Enoch in the Old Testament. He's one of those "forerunners" who highlighted the kind of life God wanted for His people all along.

"Enoch lived 365 years, walking in close fellowship with God. Then one day he disappeared because God took him." Genesis 5:23, 24 NLT

Could it be a coincidence that he lived 365 years? I am childlike enough to believe that it's not! We live much shorter lives now, but his 365 years of walking in close fellowship with God signal to me that God intends to give us that kind of relationship with Him 365 days a year. 24/7. We *can* live in close fellowship with God. Wow—what a promise! As an exclamation point on this kind of life, he was one of the two (Enoch and Elijah) who were "beamed up" and didn't taste death! Maybe it was to show us the importance of walking in close fellowship with God, day in and day out. This was as miraculous as Elijah's dramatic life full of signs and wonders. Both are equally important. Both are examples of living an Immanuel Life.

We have so much more available than those two did! Jesus inaugurated a New Covenant in His blood that gave us direct access to the throne of God. Moreover, He came to live inside us— it doesn't get any closer than that!

God has provided many additional "on ramps" for us to engage with Him and walk in close fellowship with Him. We do need all the help we can get!

In the first chapter, I described a supernatural dream/vision encounter that changed my life. This is one of the ways that the Lord opens a window and lets you in to know Him more intimately. You know He's real, but He becomes "really, *really real*" when spiritual manifestations like this happen! I think they are a part of the "normal Christian life," to bring more of heaven to earth in our lives.

Sometimes others have received words of encouragement for us. It is often a "God moment" when someone speaks an "on target" word from the Lord to you without having any knowledge of your situation or what's going on inside of you.

We can engage God personally and in the community through daily prayers and devotional Bible reading, Bible studies on our own and with others, engaging in worship, being involved in a church community, and listening to the teachings of gifted leaders that God has given to His church. This is our regular spiritual food and drink.

It's my hope that you will read this book with a group of your friends and work through it together. I've done this with friends for years, and it has been a huge catalyst for growth and change in my life. I hope this will be the same for you!

The prayers I gave you at the end of each of the virtues are meant to be "door openers" for "more"—simply to initiate the process of engaging with the Lord for the work of grace to form this quality in you.

There are some especially good tools to help you in that process that I'd like to recommend to you now.

One is called Immanuel Journaling, described in the book *Joyful Journey* by E. James Wilder, Anna Kang, John and Sungshim Loppnow.[26] You can find the book on Amazon. It is a conversational journaling tool that helps you engage with God by asking Him specific questions and listening for His answers. It's based on the way that the Lord engaged with Moses at the burning bush and with Hagar when she was in distress in the wilderness. The specific questions come from these passages. I will copy a worksheet here for you to use. You can find more information at www.joystartshere.com. This is great to do on your own and with a group—I've done it both ways, and it is very powerful!

Joyful Journey
Listening to Immanuel

Immanuel Journaling Exercise: The following simple steps for seeing our lives the way God does are from *Joyful Journey* by Wilder, Kang, Loppnow and Loppnow ©2015 and used by permission. Permission granted to duplicate for personal or group use.

- STEP ONE—Gratitude. Write anything I appreciate and then write God's response to my gratitude. Dear God, I'm thankful for... *Dear child of mine...*

- STEP TWO—I can see you. *Write from God's perspective what He observes in you right now, including your physical sensations. I can see you at your desk. Your breathing is shallow, and your shoulders are tight...*

- STEP THREE—I can hear you. *Write from God's perspective what He hears you saying to yourself. You are wondering if I will speak to you and how you would ever know. You are discouraged and tire ... OR: You woke up full of energy this morning. You are ready to take on the world. Your mind is buzzing...*

- STEP FOUR—I understand how big this is for you. *How does God see your dreams? Are they blessings or upsets and troubles? I want you to know that I care about what matters to you. Your desire to*

honor me brings me great pleasure...
OR: I understand how intimidated you feel. This situation feels all-consuming to you as if you are about to sink...

- STEP FIVE—I am glad to be with you and treat your weakness tenderly. *How does God express His desire to participate in your life? Your dreams are precious to me. I fill you with life each day and really enjoy your desire to...*
OR: I see your discouragement after yelling again. Times when you are frustrated and tired are when I want to be closer to you...

- STEP SIX—I can do something about what you are going through. *What does God give you for this time? Come away with me. I offer you times of refreshing, new energy and vision...*
OR: I will strengthen you. Remember how your friend encouraged you last week? With me you are not alone...

- STEP SEVEN—Read what you have written aloud (preferably to someone.)

The above exercise is again from *Joyful Journey: Listening to Immanuel* by E. James Wilder, Anna Kang, John and Sungshim Loppnow ©2015.[27]

Please visit www.lifemodelworks.org for more.

When you need healing for your heart, I highly recommend Immanuel Healing Prayer. You can find help for this kind of prayer under the Bonus Resources tab at this website: https://joystartshere.com; click the Resources tab, then Bonus Resources. You will find there: Immanuel Healing: God With Us by E. James Wilder.[28] I did this powerful healing prayer with Rev. Kitty Wilder when I went through my "Job" season, and it was life changing for me. I do this kind of prayer regularly when I need it and have also done it with many others. It is something that you can learn to do with your home group or fellowship to keep current in your relationship with the Lord. We live in a world full of trials, and we sometimes lose step with the spirit and need to get back on track. This is not the only way to re-engage with the Lord and receive healing, but it is the one I have found most powerful and effective in my own life.

I recommend the books *Joyful Journey: Listening to Immanuel*[29] and *Living From the Heart Jesus Gave You*[30] which you can find on Amazon and www.joystartshere.com. They are excellent resources for living an Immanuel Lifestyle.

****

As you read this book and identify where you are now and what area the Lord is emphasizing in your life now, take the first step—enter the dance! Develop your relationship with the Lord to the place where your thoughts and His are engaged throughout the day. Listen and know His voice. Let your conversation with Him become a two-way street, not a monologue. Never give up. Just DANCE!

Epilogue
A PROMISE FROM THE LORD FOR YOU

As I was writing this book and coming under the pressure to get so many things done by a certain time, I had a night where I came under a huge swirl of accusing, shaming thoughts. Thoughts like, "You're a failure, you will let everyone down, you didn't do this or that right, you should be ashamed of yourself, you'll never get this done…" I felt like there was a swarm of bees around my head that were stinging me with these thoughts. I wrestled all night, tossed and turned and couldn't sleep. The lower half of my body was hot, the upper half of my body was covered with a cold sweat, and I was shaking when I woke up.

The next morning, I got my friends praying and prayed with my husband and did okay during the day. That night, I went to a home group Bible study where we studied the parable of the prodigal son. It was a wonderful time of sharing and insights, of being washed by God's Word; the Holy Spirit was definitely guiding us all. I shared about the shame both sons felt, one for his bad behavior, the other for his 'performance trap' mindset. I shared about the Jewish tradition of the scapegoat that was ceremonially burdened with all the shame of the people and then sent to the wilderness to wander and die in isolation. I marveled once again that the Lord Jesus Himself then became the scapegoat on the cross to carry away all our shame once and for all.

That night, the Lord came to me in a dream as the scapegoat. The goat spoke and said, "I've come to take away all your shame." I recognized the Lord's voice and felt His Presence. Then I was taken into a memory of something that happened in my school lunchroom when I was eight years old. It was in a little, rural elementary school in Ohio where I attended first through third grades.

In the memory, I was in the lunch line, being silly and frisky, laughing with friends. I was shaking hands with one of my girlfriends, jumping up and down a bit. Suddenly the school principal came up and grabbed my arm, jerking me out of the line. She was a sour-looking, stern, spinster lady, probably a bitter woman, someone the kids would avoid. She dragged me over to the other side of the lunchroom and made me sit by myself with my back to the other children. She said, "You could've made someone spill their lunch tray! What were you thinking? You should be ashamed of yourself! You're going to sit here by yourself until lunch is over."

I was mortified and so very embarrassed. My little face was hot with shame. It was wintertime, so I had my snow pants on that day, and as I sat there at the table, my legs were burning up. My upper body had broken out in a cold sweat, and I was shaking. My face was buried in my arms, head down on the table. I was frozen there for the whole lunch period, my mind swarming with accusatory, shaming thoughts. When the bell rang, I got up and went to class under a cloud of shame. I went home on the school bus, sat by myself, and stared out the window the whole time. I never said a word to my parents or to anyone about it; I just buried it.

Through the years, I know my husband Michael and I talked about this. But I pretty much thought there wasn't a reason to pray through this memory for healing. I just thought it was water under the dam, ancient history. But the Lord was clearly coming to me in this dream to say, "You have a pocket of shame here, a stronghold that got set up in a traumatic event in your childhood. I'm here to take away all your shame." So, the next morning Michael and I prayed together, an Immanuel healing prayer (described in chapter ten).

In our prayer time, I first thanked the Lord for coming to me in the dream. He responded and said, "I'm so happy to finally be 'going there' in this memory with you." I asked the Lord where He was when this was happening to me. He showed me that He was sitting right beside me on the side bench of that table, facing me. He was looking at me with eyes of deep compassion and had a tear running down His cheek. I sensed Him there and found the courage to lift up my little eight-year-old head and look at him. I felt so very small and so very diminished by what was happening to me. As I looked at him, tears started rolling down my face, and I said to him, "How can you, the big God of all heaven and earth, care about little me and my little pains?" He looked at me with even more compassion in His eyes and then opened up His chest to reveal His heart. It was surrounded by the crown of thorns that was once upon His head, each thorn piercing his heart with little drops of blood dripping from each one. I knew He was feeling every one of my pains, no matter how small. He let His own heart feel and bear them all. He said, "Oh my darling Terri, all your 'littles' are so very BIG to me." He repeated it three times, each time with more love and more emotion. I believed Him! I received that! I sobbed and sobbed until I couldn't sob any more. As I did, all of my shame went out of me into Him.

In the prayer time, when I was done crying, I got up and walked by the principal and said to her, "I forgive you." Then I went out to rejoin my friends and started playing and laughing again like nothing had happened. This is how the Immanuel healing prayer time ended.

Wow! I felt clean and I was free. There had been a stronghold there in my life that gave the enemy access to harass and shame me when that 'perfect storm' happened as I was finishing this book. It was exposed, and I gave the Lord access to this ground in my life and was set free!

The Lord said, "This is the kind of thing that will happen for the women who will read this book. Things that perhaps they thought weren't an issue will suddenly be exposed and there will be an opportunity to invite me in to set them free. And if I set them free, they will be free indeed!"

"So if the Son sets you free, you will be free indeed." John 8:36 ESV

About the Author

Terri Sullivant is a **Fully Alive** woman who has been dancing gracefully with God for many years. As a minister, pastor, speaker, friend, and coach, she inspires and teaches young and old alike how to enter their own dance with the Divine. She speaks vulnerably about her struggles and trials as she testifies to the breakthroughs she has made and the ground she has gained. She is the co-founder with her husband, Michael, of  Radius Ministries, New Hope Community, and the proprietor of Fully Alive Coaching. Through these avenues, Terri is witnessing the transformation of many lives by the practical applications of heavenly grace, presence, and power. She is the mother of five happily married children and a growing flock of grandchildren. You can contact her using the contact forms on her websites, and make sure to sign up for her blog while you're at it!

http://radius-group.org or
http://radiusministries.org - Radius Ministries website
http://fullyalive5.com - Fully Alive Coaching website

Appendix A:
DISCUSSION POINTS/QUESTIONS

I have included some discussion points/questions for you to use on your own or for group study with this book. It's helpful if everyone in the group reads the book before beginning. On both of my websites, www.radius-group.org and www.fullyalive5.com (under the products tab under "free stuff"), I have a study guide for participants and one for facilitators available to download. The study guide has the chapters divided up for a 7-week study. This should help everyone stay in sync as you read and study this book together.

Chapter 1 The Encounter
- How did reading about this Encounter impact you?
- What God-encounters of your own have you had? Please share!
- What does "being fully me with Jesus in me" mean to you?
- What are your thoughts about the "grace-gift exchange"?
- Envision the woman in the last part of the encounter, the Fully Alive Woman—describe what she looks like to you.

- Using the analogy of physical alignment (spinal), describe the difference between a healthy and unhealthy alignment: a) with Jesus; b) within yourself; c) with other people.

Chapter 2 The Backstory
- If you were to draw a timeline of your life, what key points would you include?
- If you/your group desires, use an online or printable timeline, e.g. https://www.timetoast.com/timelines/183970, Use this to reflect on your life, get more in touch with your story, and tell your stories to your group.

Chapter 3 The BETTER WAY (aka *The Radical Middle*)
- What are your thoughts about the definition of the BETTER WAY/ Radical Middle presented in this chapter?
- As you read the section on the CROSS, what are your reflections?
- Specifically, what's your personal situation regarding the dilemma described in the section on the BETTER WAY: the Vocation of Virtuous Women? What does love look like for everyone concerned in your life, including you?

Chapter 4 The Invitation
- What dancers have you seen that depicted the kind of oneness described in the first part of this chapter?
- What fears, if any, do you have about entering this dance?
- On a scale of one to ten, ten being "fully alive" and one being "mostly dead," what's your perception of where you are in your life right now?
- The three core desires of a woman described in the book *Captivating* are: to be romanced, to play an irreplaceable role in a great adventure, and to unveil beauty. Take a moment to reflect on each one. Which of these do you feel has been fulfilled in your heart? Where do you feel

your heart may have shut down/given up? Pray through this with your friends/study group until your heart opens up again.

- What image does the Virtuous Woman described in Proverbs 31 evoke in you?
- How do the 28 virtues described in this encounter impact you?

Chapter 5 The Virtues Part 1 (Fruits of the Spirit)

- Reminder list: Unfailing Love, Merry Heart, Peaceful Tranquility, Lady Longsuffering, Loving Kindness, Shirley Goodness, Faithful and True, Gentle and Meek, Ms. Temperance
- Which of these nine virtues stood out most to you?
- Describe how the virtue you've chosen affects your life at this time.
- What would you need to let go of right now to receive something you value more, i.e. the gift God is offering you?
- Pray out loud the prayer in the book associated with the grace-gift you are receiving. If you are doing this in a group, pray with and for each person. Be sure to journal this—make it a "memorial stone"—date it and keep it. Stay with it until this area is securely rooted in your life.
- When the Lord emphasizes another grace-gift He wants to give you, go through the same process.

Chapter 6 The Virtues Part 2 (Relationships/Roles)

- Reminder list: Beloved Daughter, Mama Bear, Precious Bride, Soul Sister, Faithful Friend
- Which one of these, if any, was highlighted to you?
- What is happening in your life right now that sets the stage for receiving this grace-gift?
- What might you need to release to make room for it?
- Pray out loud the prayer in the book associated with the grace-gift you are receiving. If you are doing this in a group, pray with and for each person. Be sure to journal this—make it a "memorial stone"—date it and keep it. Stay with it until this area is securely rooted in your life.

- When the Lord emphasizes another grace-gift He wants to give you, go through the same process.

Chapter 7 The Virtues Part 3 (Qualities of Nobility)
- Reminder list: Lady Pure Heart, Divine Forgiveness, Maid of Honor, The Lord's Princess, Del Gratia, Regina
- Imagine the Lord in His royal robe, standing before you with a scepter. As He extends the scepter to bless you, which of these titles is He bestowing on you?
- Why do you think He is offering this to you right now?
- What lesser "title" would you need to give up to receive this new one?
- Pray out loud the prayer in the book associated with the grace-gift you are receiving. If you are doing this in a group, pray with and for each person. Be sure to journal this—make it a "memorial stone"—date it and keep it. Stay with it until this area is securely rooted in your life.
- When the Lord emphasizes another grace-gift He wants to give you, go through the same process.

Chapter 8 The Virtues Part 4 (Character Strengths)
- Reminder list: Fearlessly Courageous, Personality Plus, Total Security, Graceful Dancer, Timeless Beauty, Grateful (Appreciated), Job's Sister, Unsinkable Hope, Passionate Sage
- Which of these nine character strengths confirmed something the Lord has on the "front burner" in your life right now?
- Why is this on the "front burner" now, in your understanding?
- What would you need to relinquish in order to free up the space needed to receive this grace-gift?
- Pray out loud the prayer in the book associated with the grace-gift you are receiving. If you are doing this in a group, pray with and for each person. Be sure to journal this—make it a "memorial stone"—date it and keep it. Stay with it until this area is securely rooted in your life.

- When the Lord emphasizes another grace-gift He wants to give you, go through the same process.

Chapter 9 The Finale–The Fully Alive Woman

- Read through the encounter again—it is repeated in this chapter. What do you notice this time that you may not have the first time you read it?
- Go to this part of the chapter and do the visualization exercise: "Take a deep breath now and close your eyes. Visualize YOURSELF as that woman. Put your face in the picture I just described..." What do you see? Share it!
- Look at the declaration in big bold letters—say it or shout it out loud!
- Write down the "statement of faith" in the space provided or in your journal. Date it. Keep it safe. Come back to it and say it again and again, visualizing yourself as "that woman." You are HER! Repeat these as often as you can!
- A good friend of mine, Janet Johns, who was one of the first women to hear about this encounter, really personalized it—she had a painting made with her face on it as the Fully Alive Woman! She still has it to this day, for over 20 years now. Consider doing something like this— either a sketch or whatever else would be meaningful to you—so that you can personalize it and "make it your own!"

Chapter 10 Where Are You Now?

- The Lord's Prayer: For those of you who would like to come into relationship with Jesus Christ, follow the prayer like "stepping stones" of faith. If you'd like, let me know about it via the contact form at http://radius-group.org. Make sure to get involved with a healthy, vibrant church near you, and tell any Christian friends you may know that you have invited Jesus into your life and surrendered yours to Him. Welcome to the Dance!
- The Secrets to Spiritual Growth: What seems to be your need at the moment? Which spiritual disciplines are you currently doing? Which

would you want to add? How might you be intentional about doing them?

- The Immanuel Life—read the description of the Immanuel Life. Feel free to use the tools provided in this section. There are many others, but these are ones I have found particularly helpful to do on your own or with a group.

*Additional Discussion Points from quotes in the book:

- *True spirituality is not about religion; it's about relationship.*
- *The divine invitation beckons you to come and dance on the rooftops of life with our Savior, becoming one with him in His thoughts, feelings, actions—just like a healthy relationship between a husband and wife, only MORE. Much more.*
- *It seems to me that finding the "radical middle," the BETTER WAY, rather than negotiating a compromise, is really about knowing what love looks like for you and all the people you care about in your situation. It's about honoring the truth on all sides of an issue and coming up higher to where love is. It's about seeking to keep the relationships bigger than the problem.*
- *Whatever you choose to focus on will be magnified in your eyes.*
- *Wisdom comes from syncing with Me as you metabolize and synthesize both beauty and pain.*

Appendix B:
NEXT STEPS

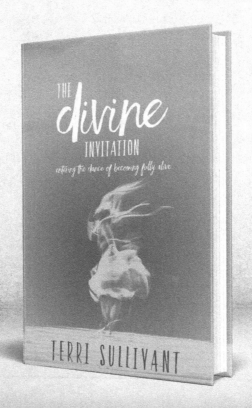

Endnotes

1. "Imprinting", Britannica.com, https://www.britannica.com/topic/imprinting, accessed Feb. 10, 2017

2. Quote from Bill Johnson found on Google Images: https://goo.gl/images/WxCmjL, accessed Feb. 10, 2017

3. Bill Jackson, *The Quest for the Radical Middle: a History of the Vineyard;* (Vineyard International Publishing, July 14, 1999)

4. *Fiddler on the Roof,* a Norman Jewison film, 1971, United Artists Corp.

5. Eldredge, John; Eldredge, Stasi (2011-04-17). *Captivating,* Revised and Updated: (Chapter 1, p. 8). Thomas Nelson.

6. Quote from Frederick Brotherton Meyer, Quotes Daddy https://www.quotesdaddy.com/quote/1400704/frederick-brotherton-meyer-english-keswick-movement-evangelist/joy-is-peace-dancing-peace-is-joy-at-rest, accessed June. 10, 2017

7. From the book, *The Life Model,* by Dr. Jim Wilder quoted by the Fathering Leadership Blog dated December 9, 2010 by Robert Hartzell: https://www.roberthartzell.com/fathers-love-defaulting-to-joy/, accessed June 10, 2017

8. Wilder, E.James PhD; Kang, Anna; Loppnow,John; Loppnow, Sungshim; *Joyful Journey,* Shepherd's House Inc., 2015, Chapter 3, Kindle edition

9. Def. of kindness/https://en.wikipedia.org/wiki/Kindness, accessed June 15, 2017

10. Def. of faithfulness, https://en.wikipedia.org/wiki/Faithfulness, accessed June 15, 2017

11. Self Control/Psychology today online, https://www.psychologytoday.com/basics/self-control, accessed June 15, 2017

12. http://aboverubies.org/index.php/2013-11-12-17-55-51/english-language/motherhood/2310-motherhood-motherhood-quotes-no-3

13. Friedrich Nietzsche Quotes. BrainyQuote.com, Xplore Inc, 2017. https://www.brainyquote.com/quotes/quotes/f/friedrichn109784.html, accessed August 29, 2017.

14. Matthew Arnold, 19th c poet/philosopher, https://www.goodreads.com/quotes/413325

15. Thomas Aquinas Quotes. BrainyQuote.com, Xplore Inc, 2017. https://www.brainyquote.com/quotes/quotes/t/thomasaqui163328.html, accessed August 30, 2017.

16. http://www.finestquotes.com/movie_quotes/movie/Its+a+Wonderful+Life/page/0.htm, accessed August 27, 2017

17. Baker, Lisa Jo, *Never Unfriended,* Nashville, TN, B & H Publishing Group, 2017, Kindle Edition

18. "Nobility", definition, https://www.merriam-webster.com/dictionary/nobility; accessed August 30, 2017

19. Alexander Pope Quotes. BrainyQuote.com, Xplore Inc, 2017. https://www.brainyquote.com/quotes/quotes/a/alexanderp101451.html, Accessed August 27, 2017

20. "Forgiveness", definition, https://en.wikipedia.org/wiki/Forgiveness; accessed August 30, 2017

21. Lewis, CS; https://www.values.com/inspirational-quotes/6940

22. Beth Moore quote listed on the Amazon.com webpage promoting Beth Moore's book *So Long Insecurity*: https://www.amazon.com/So-Long-Insecurity-Youve-Friend/dp/1414334737

23. Carly Simon Quotes. BrainyQuote.com, Xplore Inc, 2017. https://www.brainyquote.com/quotes/quotes/c/carlysimon261072.html, accessed August 27, 2017.

24. Ten Boom, Corrie, *The Hiding Place* (New York: Random House 1982)

25. Written by Tia Sillers, Mark Sanders • Copyright © Sony/ATV Music Publishing LLC, Universal Music Publishing Group

26. Wilder, E.James PhD; Kang, Anna; Loppnow,John; Loppnow, Sungshim; *Joyful Journey,* Shepherd's House Inc., 2015

27. This exercise is from *Joyful Journey: Listening to Immanuel* by E. James Wilder, Anna Kang, John and Sungshim Loppnow ©2015.

28. https://joystartshere.com/bonus-resources/, Click 'bonus resources' tab and go to *Immanuel Healing: God With Us,* by E. James Wilder, PhD, and click the download button

29. E. James Wilder, Anna Kang, John and Sungshim Loppnow, *Joyful Journey: Listening to Immanuel,* ©2015, Shepherd's House, Inc.

30. Freisen, James G.,PhD, E. James Wilder, PhD, Bierling, Ann M, M.A., Koepcke, Rick, M.A., and Poole, Maribeth, M.A., *Living From the Heart Jesus Gave You,* copyright 1999, 2000, 2004, 2010, 2013, Shepherd's House, Inc.

Morgan James
Speakers Group

www.TheMorganJamesSpeakersGroup.com

We connect Morgan James published
authors with live and online events
and audiences who will benefit
from their expertise.

Printed in the USA
CPSIA information can be obtained
at www.ICGtesting.com
JSHW022342140824
68134JS00019B/1637